The Gift of Loving-Kindness *skillfully guides us to train our minds and hearts in the practice of loving-kindness meditation. The meditative exercises in this book can spark one's journey into greater love and compassion or enrich it anywhere along the path. Combining internal reflection and mindful exploration of our heart's capacity, these pragmatic exercises open us to genuine transformation.*

—Sharon Salzberg, author of *Lovingkindness: The Revolutionary Art of Happiness*

Keep The Gift of Loving-Kindness *on your bed table and let its wisdom guide you. This book offers a rich assortment of contemplations that will open and free your heart.*

—Tara Branch, Buddhist teacher and author of *Radical Acceptance: Embracing your Life with the Heart of a Buddha*

Simply reading these words will awaken you. Actually doing even one of these practices could profoundly transform your life. I offer warm and deep thanks to the authors for blessing us with these hundred doorways to the deepest and best parts of ourselves as human beings.

—Jeffrey Brantley, MD, author of *Calming Your Anxious Mind*

Use this practical and heartfelt book to discover how to open your heart in any circumstance. New scientific evidence confirms that filling your heart with loving-kindness can broaden your mind and build your best possible future.

—Barbara L. Fredrickson, Ph.D., recipient of the Templeton Positive Psychology Prize

the gift of loving-kindness

100 Mindful Practices

for Compassion, Generosity

& Forgiveness

mary brantley & tesilya hanauer

New Harbinger Publications, Inc.

Publisher's Note

This publication is designed to provide accurate and authoritative information in regard to the subject matter covered. It is sold with the understanding that the publisher is not engaged in rendering psychological, financial, legal, or other professional services. If expert assistance or counseling is needed, the services of a competent professional should be sought.

Distributed in Canada by Raincoast Books

Copyright © 2008 by Mary Brantley and Tesilya Hanauer
New Harbinger Publications, Inc.
5674 Shattuck Avenue
Oakland, CA 94609
www.newharbinger.com

Cover design by Amy Shoup; Text design by Amy Shoup and Michele Waters-Kermes; Acquired by Melissa Kirk

Library of Congress Cataloging-in-Publication Data

Brantley, Mary.
  The gift of loving-kindness : 100 meditations on compassion, forgiveness, and generosity / Mary Brantley and Tesilya Hanauer.
    p. cm.
  ISBN-13: 978-1-57224-562-4 (pbk. : alk. paper)
  ISBN-10: 1-57224-562-X (pbk.)
  1. Sympathy. 2. Compassion. 3. Forgiveness. 4. Generosity. 5. Meditation. I. Hanauer, Tesilya II. Title.
  BF575.S9B73 2008
  177'.7--dc22
                                    2008027636

10   09   08

10   9   8   7   6   5   4   3   2   1   First printing

To my husband, Jeff, for his love, wisdom, and heartfelt support, and for the blessings of our twenty-six years of marriage.

—MB

To Lua, Ryan, Zeya, Lucan, Rainier, Luna Trinity, and all the other children in my life. May you always know you are loved.

—TH

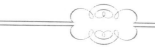

Contents

Acknowledgments . . . xi

Introduction to Loving-Kindness Meditation . . . 1

What Is Loving-Kindness? . . . 2

An Ancient Practice . . . 5

What Loving-Kindness Meditation Is Not . . . 7

Why We Wrote This Book . . . 8

Fundamental Qualities of Loving-Kindness Meditation . . . 22

How to Use This Book . . . 28

Basic Instruction for Loving-Kindness Meditation . . . 30

Instructions for Formal Loving-Kindness Meditation . . . 33

Instructions for Informal Loving-Kindness Meditation . . . 40

PART ONE: Loving-Kindness Toward Yourself . . . 43

Introduction . . . 44

Be Your Own Friend – 50 • Loving-Kindness Toward Your Body – 52 • Formal Peaceful Walking Meditation – 54 • Informal Peaceful Walking Meditation – 56 • Follow the Ocean Waves – 58 • Take Kindness for a Drive – 60 • Remember Kindness in Your Family – 62 • Beach Walk – 64 • Forgive Yourself – 66 • Melt the Ice – 68 • Love Travels Like the Wind – 70 • Find a Safe Harbor – 72 • Love on the Go – 74 • Give Yourself a Present – 76 • Notice Your Small Acts of Kindness – 78 • Count On Support – 80 • May You Be Happy – 82 • Let the Light In – 84 • Accept Yourself – 86 • Clear Your Heart – 88 • Find a Friend in You – 90 • Tap into the Force of Kindness – 92 • Kindness Is a Choice – 94 • Breathe in Joy – 96 • Things That Make You Feel Good – 98 • Calm in the Face of Change – 100

PART TWO: Loving-Kindness Toward Difficult Emotions . . . 103

Introduction . . . 104

Befriend the Difficult – 110 • Be Still – 112 • Don't Look Back – 114 • Accept the Task – 116 • Stop the Struggle – 118 • Write a New Story – 120 • Take a Fear Break – 122 • Befriend the Monsters – 124 • Let Your Shadow Walk in Front of You – 126 • More Joy, Please – 128 • Raw Beauty – 130 • Let the Clouds Pass Over – 132 • Meet Anger with Kindness – 134 • Awaken the Goodness Within You – 136 • A Day of Heartfulness – 138 • Drop the Weight – 140 • Bow to Your Anger – 142 • Balance Your Emotions – 144 • Break Old Habits – 146 • Spark Your Happiness – 148 • Only Boring People Get Bored – 150 • Open the Box of Love – 152 • When the Cheese Drives You Nuts – 154 • Balance on the Waves – 156 • Monster Mind – 158 • When the Party Is Over – 160

PART THREE: Loving-Kindness Toward Others . . . 163

Introduction . . . 164

Behold the Mystery – 170 • Friendship Power – 172 • We Are Family – 174 • Be Kind to Your Neighbors – 176 • Wish Them Well – 178 • Appreciate the Challenger – 180 • Thank You, Teacher – 182 • Share Your Happiness – 184 • A Friend in Need – 186 • Random Acts of Gratitude – 188 • Open the Door to Your Heart – 190 • The Wishing Well – 192 • Friendship to Spare – 194 • Your Mother's Kindness – 196 • See Your Father's Goodness – 198 • We All Make Mistakes – 200 • Offering Kindness to a Friend – 202 • Rays of Goodness – 204 • Meet Anger with Love – 206 • The Generous Heart Gives – 208 • Envy No More – 210 • The Mindful Minute – 212 • Let Kindness Steer Your Mind – 214

PART FOUR: Extending Loving-Kindness Toward the World . . . 217
Introduction . . . 218

It's Expensive to Get Sick – 224 • Open Your Heart to a Soldier – 226
• Remember Your Goodness – 228 • Compassion Toward a Loved One
– 230 • Generosity in Your Town – 232 • Loving Creatures – 234
• Be Happy – 236 • People Watching – 238 • Travel in Kindness
– 240 • Stranger or Friend? – 242 • Plant Love – 244 • See the
Good – 246 • Forgive Those Who Have Trespassed Against You – 248
• Open Your Heart Like a Flower to the Sun – 250 • Do No Harm
– 252 • May We Be at Ease – 253 • Your Brother on the Street – 254
• Cultivate the Garden of Your Mind – 256 • Get on the Kind Bus
– 258 • An End to Suffering – 260 • Three Paths to Letting
Go – 262 • Caught in the Web of Love – 264 • Be a Lover, Not a
Fighter – 266 • Soften Your Heart – 268 • Love Your Enemy – 270
• Wrapped Up in Your Love – 272

Conclusion . . . 275
Going Forward . . . 276
Resources . . . 279

Acknowledgments

We'd like to acknowledge Sharon Salzberg for blazing the trail of loving-kindness in the West. She has been at the frontier of teaching and practicing loving-kindness for decades. Without her work, and the work of her teachers before her, this book would not exist. Thank you.

Introduction to Loving-Kindness Meditation

What Is Loving-Kindness?

Loving-kindness means great friendliness to self and others. Loving-kindness meditation, which fosters the growth and development of this quality of being, is easy to learn. Practicing loving-kindness sheds light on our own innate goodness. Kindness and compassion are qualities that live within all of us. You don't buy them or own them—you live them. Loving-kindness practice helps develop positive feelings and lets us embrace all aspects of ourselves and others unconditionally. It fosters a self-discovery that teaches us how to be a true friend to ourselves and others, and shows us how to meet our inner critic with love instead of hate.

The simplest explanation of loving-kindness meditation is that you repeat a series of phrases aimed at yourself, a loved one, a person you feel neutral about, a difficult person, and, finally, all living things, with the intention of generating great friendliness for yourself and others. For example, you might direct the following loving-kindness phrases toward yourself:

May I be happy.

May I be healthy.

May I be peaceful.

May I be safe.

Of course, there's more to it than that, and in the following pages we'll explain the intricacies of this meditation practice.

In *Loving-Kindness: The Revolutionary Art of Happiness* (Shambhala, 1995), Sharon Salzberg writes that by practicing loving-kindness we learn to cultivate the good—meaning we discover the incredible power of love present within each of us. She goes on to say that in order to access this power, we must overcome our limited view of our own potential and rediscover a more expansive view of what is possible for us.

Salzberg believes this can be achieved and sustained through spiritual practice. This book is an invitation to practice that kindness toward yourself and others.

Loving-kindness meditation as we present it is not only a technique, it's also a way to approach life. It can help you break mental habits of meanness and self-judgment, and it allows your mind to rest from the everyday push and pull of the past and the future. This practice has the potential to make you feel safe and at ease inside your own skin.

At times, life may be stressful, relationships difficult, or health worrisome. Loving-kindness gives you a way to have a different relationship to fears from within and threats from outside. The most inspiring aspect of this practice is how it reveals that you already harbor a place of peace and great strength within. You just have to wake it up. The exercises in this book will help you do that.

Loving-kindness is all-inclusive; it leaves no one out of your heart. Greatness of heart is a feeling we can all cultivate. Loving-kindness meditation is a road map for how to be in the world and how to experience inner peace and happiness.

An Ancient Practice

Loving-kindness meditation, sometimes called *metta*, or *maitri*, meditation, is an ancient practice that comes from the teachings of the Buddha. It is said that the Buddha first taught this meditation as an antidote to fear. According to legend, he was in a forest with a group of monks, and sent them off to meditate. The forest was full of tree spirits who resented the monks coming into their territory. When night fell, the tree spirits scared the monks by making loud noises, creating bad smells, and appearing as ghoulish figures. The monks ran back to the Buddha asking to be sent someplace else to meditate.

The Buddha instructed the monks in loving-kindness meditation. The legend ends with the monks going back into the forest and practicing loving-kindness. It is said that the tree spirits were so touched by the loving energy that filled the forest, they ended up caring for and serving the monks.

Although this form of meditation comes from Buddhist tradition, you certainly don't have to be Buddhist to practice it or benefit from it. The qualities of friendliness, kindness, and compassion are compatible with all faith traditions and reside in all human beings.

What Loving-Kindness Meditation Is Not

Loving-kindness should not be confused with the common experiences of love. The word "love" itself can be confusing, and in Western culture it's often tied up with attachment and desire. There's nothing wrong in wanting things—everyone wants something. But is that love?

The love we're describing in this book is inner friendliness, expressed by being kind toward ourselves and finding the good in others. We all have loving qualities inside us, but most of us have to learn how to tap into that inner goodness. This book will help you do that.

Why We Wrote This Book

This book is the outgrowth of our spiritual practice. We started this project as two strangers who were both influenced by loving-kindness. Our shared interest in the topic led us to write this book together, a testament to the power of loving-kindness to show us the ways in which we are all interconnected.

Mary's Journey

I had been meditating for many years, but it was not until I took a ten-day silent meditation retreat with Sharon Salzberg and Joseph Goldstein in February 1991 that I had my first experience with loving-kindness meditation. It was cold there in Barre, Massachusetts. Everything was covered in a blanket of snow. We would wake up to snow falling and go to bed with it still falling. The snow gave the land a majestic quality; everything looked so peaceful. It was the perfect setting to practice kindness.

After being told to sit comfortably, we were given one of our first loving-kindness meditation instructions: to send loving-kindness phrases to ourselves—for example, "May I have mental happiness." At first, I had the same reaction that so many others say they've had to this: I felt selfish. I felt like I should be sending kind wishes to someone else first.

As the days rolled on, I saw that my heart was not really open to myself. I was holding on to old stories filled with self-blame and self-judgment. However, by the end of the retreat Sharon and Joseph had guided us with their deep wisdom, and I began to understand that if you can't be kind to yourself, it's very hard to fully love others. This retreat was very profound and awakened something inside of me.

Every year since then, I've taken a meditation retreat—ranging from seven to ten days—mostly at Insight Meditation Society in Barre, Massachusetts, with various teachers. The instructors' dedication to a life of meditation practice has had a huge influence on my life. They have been my role models for how to live, and they have always communicated that the wisdom in the various meditation teachings must come from my own experience.

Because it isn't rooted in blind faith, one of the beauties of loving-kindness meditation is that you can be affiliated with any religion or no religion. Anyone can practice kindness.

At home, my husband, Jeff, and I began to open our house on Sunday mornings to anyone interested in meditating with a group. Jeff would often read something inspirational, and then we would sit in silence and meditate. I began to end these gatherings with a loving-kindness meditation, which was my first experience with conveying what I had learned about loving-kindness to others. Little did I know at the time, that was just the beginning of something that would shape my life.

More opportunities arose for me to bring loving-kindness meditation forward. In 2000, I was invited to be an instructor for the Mindfulness-Based Stress Reduction program at Duke University Medical Center, Duke Integrative Medicine. Modeled after Jon Kabat-Zinn's work at the University of Massachusetts Medical Center, it's an eight-week program dedicated to teaching people how to be present in their lives using mindfulness meditation and yoga.

The core attitudes of the program are nonjudging, patience, trust, nonstriving, acceptance, and letting go.

At Duke I recorded a CD explaining and guiding loving-kindness meditation, and I taught an eight-week "graduate" course in loving-kindness meditation. (The graduate course is open to anyone who has completed the eight-week foundation program in mindfulness-based stress reduction.) The goal of the loving-kindness meditation class is to deepen one's experience of this practice and explore in greater depth how compassion, forgiveness, equanimity, and generosity might be cultivated in one's life. It's been a privilege and an honor to work with the people who come through our programs.

Another chance to foster loving-kindness meditation began with an online business: the making and selling of unique prayer beads, which are strung while reciting loving-kindness meditation phrases for the recipient. Each strand has four main beads that represent the four wishes of loving-kindness meditation; as we string each bead, we recite the loving-kindness prayer for the person who will receive the strand.

I developed this business (www.seedsofkindness.biz) with two close friends, Gail Seybolt and Rebecca Elliott. We are all practicing psychotherapists, and we've shared our professional and spiritual lives for the last two decades. We all have a love for nature, spending many hours in our individual gardens and taking road trips together to visit beautiful gardens and explore nurseries.

The prayer bead enterprise started with an act of kindness from Gail. My husband, Jeff, and I share a birthday. Around that time, I went to my mailbox and found a package from Gail. I opened it to find a box for Jeff and me inside. As I opened my little box, a beautiful, shiny strand of beads fell out.

At first I thought it was jewelry. The card my friend wrote explained the gift: As each bead had been strung, she had repeated the loving-kindness phrases.

Her gift immediately gave me the feeling of being loved, of being deeply held in Gail's heart and prayers. Many years before, Gail had come to our house on Sundays and I had taught her loving-kindness meditation. Now my work was coming back to me, as a literal touchstone.

That was a difficult time in my life. My only brother had been diagnosed with lung cancer. Gail understood what a deep and tragic loss his death would be for me. My brother and I had a very special relationship; we held a deep respect for each other. Our parents had died, his wife had passed away, and we had learned to turn toward each other for support.

The thought of losing my brother was devastating. The beautiful prayer beads were a very timely and welcome gift.

Soon after I received her present, Gail began teaching Rebecca and me how to make the prayer beads. We both started making them and offering them as gifts. We'd give them to people during difficult times—sickness, loss, mourning—as well as for joyful events, such as weddings, births, promotions, and long trips.

We received letters and e-mails from recipients telling us how strongly they felt our kindness and prayers. The impact that the beads and the loving-kindness meditation had on people was astounding to us. Before we knew it, we'd started a new business venture: Seeds of Kindness.

In 2006 my husband and I planned a trip to Hawaii to celebrate our twenty-fifth wedding anniversary. We arranged for a layover in San Francisco so Jeff could meet his editors at New Harbinger Publications, the Oakland-based company that publishes his books.

He had never met them and this seemed like an ideal opportunity. Jeff had just finished working on the second edition of his first book, *Calming Your Anxious Mind*, and now he was writing the fourth book in New Harbinger's *Five Good Minutes* series: *Five Good Minutes with the One You Love*, with Wendy Millstine.

Before we left for our trip, Jeff carefully picked out a number of Seeds of Kindness prayer beads to give to his editors as a way of thanking them for all their hard work. One of those editors was Tesilya Hanauer, who had worked on the *Five Good Minutes* series with Jeff.

I had no idea at the time that she had previously had a profound experience with loving-kindness meditation (see "Tesilya's Journey"). I enjoyed meeting Tesilya and spending time with her in the brief period we were together.

A few months later she contacted me and asked if I would be interested in writing a book together about loving-kindness meditation. I felt honored. I also felt profoundly touched that it was through Jeff's act of generosity, and his deep feelings of kindness and gratitude for his editors, that this book was to be born. It was as though the energy of loving-kindness was manifesting itself in my life.

As I reflect on this journey, I can see how embracing the practice of loving-kindness has shaped my life. Such meditation is fertile ground for seeds of profound happiness and inner wellness. May this book help bring your seeds of happiness to fruition.

Tesilya's Journey

In my final year of college I mysteriously began experiencing sharp shooting pains under my right shoulder blade. Every time I took a breath, I felt like someone was stabbing a steely knife into my shoulder. I was aware of the pain every second of the day. Since it hurt to breathe, I started taking shallower breaths, and eventually I began feeling panicky every time I took a breath. I felt like I had to fight for each gasp of air.

The physical pain began to affect my general well-being. It was so bad I considered dropping out of college with only three months left until graduation. Some good counsel from friends, a little psychotherapy, and a few academic adjustments—including taking oral exams (rather than written ones) and learning to take notes with my left, nondominant hand—kept me in school. But the pain and labored breathing continued, and my sense of panic and fear increased.

After about a year and a half of living with the pain, anxiety, and breathlessness, I started to break down. On more than one occasion I had friends sit with me while I screamed my way through the pain. I thought it was a step in the right direction to let the pain out, rather than holding it in like I had been doing for so long.

But another friend, who was taking prerequisites for medical school, thought this approach was outlandish and rushed me to the emergency room during one of my screamfests. This was the beginning of my journey to the source of the pain and anxiety.

In the hospital, medical staff took X-rays but couldn't find anything wrong. So they gave me painkillers and muscle relaxants and sent me home. Under the influence of the drugs, I was finally able to relax and breathe without pain. I spent a week curled up in a papasan chair in my living room, watching the redwood trees dance in the wind while listening to gentle music all day.

I was enthralled with this new, pain- and anxiety-free world, and would have happily remained in this drug-induced state for an eternity if not for my housemate's gentle nudging to move on—or at least move out of the living room. When the week was over, I had to find a drug-free way through the pain. Thus began my odyssey through the land of medical practitioners.

First, I went to my general practitioner, who sent me to a physical therapist (PT). To my relief the PT was able to isolate the injury as a subscapular muscle tear, which I could finally trace back to an injury I'd sustained on a river kayaking trip the year before. The PT gave me a series of strengthening exercises that involved lifting cans of soup; needless to say, it was a humbling experience for someone who had, up to that point, been running, biking, kayaking, and working as a wildland firefighter in the Klamath National Forest.

In addition to physical therapy, I sought out an osteopath, acupuncturist, and chiropractor, each of whom prescribed a different regimen. The treatment was beginning to work—the pain was slowly subsiding—but the anxiety was persistent and I still couldn't take a deep breath.

I graduated college and headed to the desert Southwest on an extended solo road trip. One of my first stops was a four-day silent vipassana meditation retreat in Nevada City, California. (Vipassana is one of India's most ancient techniques of meditation.) In the course of meditation I was able to sit with the anxiety, and feel the pain and breathe into it, rather than trying to escape it.

A few months later while in Colorado, I met a somatic therapist who, when she heard of my struggle with the anxiety and pain, recommended Jack Kornfield's book *A Path with Heart*. I immediately went out and bought it and took it with me on a weeklong journey into Canyonlands National Park in Utah. And that's where I found the power of loving-kindness meditation.

The meditations in the book helped me start to label my thoughts, rather than get caught up in them. The one that resonated most deeply with me was the loving-kindness meditation. Each morning I would rise from my tent, climb the red rocks, wrap myself in a blanket, watch the sunrise, and repeat my own versions of these loving-kindness phrases:

May I be filled with loving-kindness.

May I be healthy and strong.

May I feel calm and at ease.

May I be happy.

The phrases represented all that I longed for and felt was lacking in my life—to be healthy, strong, calm, and happy. With the phrases came a deep feeling of acceptance of myself; the struggle with my physical pain and feelings of anxiety decreased. I found myself being more gentle and loving with my own shortcomings. My thoughts were less self-critical.

I felt greater ease in my own body, and for the first time since the shoulder injury, I was able to take deep, full breaths without pain. Peacefully observing my body, I was able to watch the anxiety when it arose—and I could sit with it, rather than trying to push it away or clamp down on it.

Loving-kindness meditation became a constant companion to me over the years and continued to help me through challenging times. When Mary's husband, Jeff, gifted me with one of her prayer beads and she told me the story of reciting the loving-kindness phrases while creating them, I was deeply moved. And when it was proposed that Mary write a book based on loving-kindness, I knew I wanted to participate in the project because loving-kindness had helped me so much in my own healing. I wanted to help bring this gift of great friendliness to others.

And so began our collaboration on this book.

Fundamental Qualities of Loving-Kindness Meditation

Generosity, forgiveness, and compassion are three important qualities that support and enrich loving-kindness meditation. Generosity helps tap into kindness. Forgiveness helps to release blocks you may experience toward yourself and others. Compassion is a doorway through which to see, and have empathy for, the pain in another.

You might ask, "If I am not always generous, forgiving, or compassionate, can I still practice loving-kindness meditation?" Yes—such meditation helps cultivate these qualities.

Generosity

Generosity is a natural state of mind we all possess. It is characterized by a readiness to give and a freedom from stinginess. We often think generosity means giving something away: gifts, money, time, a service, your place in line, a parking space. That is one form. But generosity can also be as simple as saying "thank you," smiling, or opening a door for someone.

Sometimes you are the recipient of someone else's generosity. Do you remember what it feels like when a stranger smiles at you or a fellow driver stops to let you merge into traffic? Someone's simple act of generosity can bring great joy to your heart.

The spirit of magnanimous giving that is practiced through loving-kindness taps into an inner feeling of great abundance. As we cultivate that feeling within, our generosity extends out into the world. The benefits are enormous.

Forgiveness

Forgiveness means the end of resentment. Almost everyone has been hurt by someone and has hurt someone back; your own kindness and the kindness of others may be blocked by resentment left over from those past hurts. Loving-kindness can help you practice forgiveness by teaching you to open your heart to yourself and even to someone who has hurt you.

Practicing forgiveness isn't always about forgiving someone else. If your body has pain or illness, you may need to offer it forgiveness (see "Tesilya's Journey"). Sometimes you need to forgive yourself for actions you regret. Shame, self-directed anger, and self-judgment are destructive emotions—they zap your life force and energy.

Practicing loving-kindness meditation helps you let go of things that are hard to accept about yourself. With practice, you begin to forgive yourself; you begin to find release.

Compassion

Compassion is the deep awareness of the suffering of another, coupled with the wish to relieve it. It's a cornerstone of loving-kindness meditation and a key to happiness. Opening the door to compassion allows us an all-access pass to the deep well of love that exists within us and in the world.

The key to opening that door is letting go of the illusion that people are separate from each other; compassion teaches us that everyone is deeply connected to one another. It's not about feeling sorry for yourself or others. Compassion is empathy, and empathy is being sensitive to the thoughts, feelings, and experiences of others without them having to directly communicate those things to us.

One of the best role models of compassion is the Dalai Lama. A few years ago, I (Mary) had the opportunity, along with two thousand other people, to see the Dalai Lama appear at the Mind and

Life Conference in Washington, D.C. When he came out onto the stage, he stopped, faced the audience, and bowed. He was so intensely *present*; he seemed to genuinely care for the well-being of everyone in the room. When he bowed to us I felt his deep commitment to a life of compassion and kindness.

I thought that would be the highlight of the trip, but it wasn't. At the end of the conference, my husband and I walked back to our hotel. As we turned the corner, the Dalai Lama, surrounded by security guards, was getting into a big black limousine. When we got to the end of the block, the Dalai Lama's limo stopped parallel to where we stood.

My husband and I turned and instinctively bowed toward his car. The light from the street lamp lit up the window of the limo, and in that light I could see the Dalai Lama, hands together in prayer position, bowing back at us.

I may never get any closer than that to the Dalai Lama, but I felt that I walked away with a life-changing understanding of how compassion happens in the moment, and how every interaction is an opportunity to live and take action from the heart. By bowing to us, two strangers whom he didn't know, the Dalai Lama demonstrated his belief that we are all interconnected and we all—each and every one of us—deserve kindness.

How to Use This Book

This book is arranged in an easy-to-use layout, beginning with the basic instructions for loving-kindness meditation. These will help you learn, step-by-step, how to practice this meditation. After you read through the instructions, you will find directions for guided formal and informal practice.

By formal practice, we mean you're setting aside time to do nothing but meditation. Informal practice suggests ways to bring the loving-kindness meditation into your daily life. Formal meditation helps support the informal by training the mind to concentrate.

The book is divided into four sections: kindness toward yourself, kindness toward difficult emotions, kindness toward others, and sowing seeds of kindness in the world. Each section is filled with meditation exercises that will help you practice loving-kindness in everyday situations. You don't have to do all of them and you don't have to do them in any order. It's okay if some of the exercises don't appeal to you—simply practice the ones you like.

Also, we suggest loving-kindness phrases to accompany each exercise. If the ones that we've chosen don't work for you, insert your own. The idea is that the phrases should resonate from your heart and be meaningful to you. These phrases are usually said silently, but it's okay to say them aloud.

It doesn't take much time to learn loving-kindness meditation. The only challenging part will be remembering to do it. Give yourself a chance to practice as often as you can, and give yourself a chance to succeed by bringing your full attention to your meditation practice.

When you do your formal meditation, turn off your phone and eliminate any other distractions. Find a place where you can practice undisturbed for at least five—if not twenty or forty—minutes.

Strong feelings may arise when you do these exercises. You may feel tearful, sad, or full of joy. A memory may be triggered. Just allow yourself to be with the experience without judgment or criticism. Meet each experience with kindness.

Remember, you are learning to treat yourself like a good friend, and you are learning to treat yourself and others with respect and patience. May the wisdom of loving-kindness become a part of your everyday life.

Basic Instruction for Loving-Kindness Meditation

The practice always starts with developing a loving acceptance toward yourself first and then toward others. There are different ways you can invoke feelings of kindness. The simplest way is to repeat phrases to yourself, either silently in your head or out loud, that are kind, friendly, and loving. For example, you might repeat the following four main phrases (or create your own if these don't resonate with you):

May I be happy.

May I be healthy.

May I be peaceful.

May I be safe.

Another way is to visualize yourself or someone you care about looking happy, healthy, at peace. And one more approach is to reflect on qualities of kindness, generosity, or compassion in your-self or another.

When you practice loving-kindness meditation, you will be directing phrases to the following five groups:

1   *Yourself.* You begin by directing loving-kindness toward yourself. If we don't know how to feel kindness toward ourselves, we won't be able to generate this feeling for others.

2   *A loved one,* such as a family member, good friend, teacher, or mentor. This should be someone whom you love dearly. When you think of this person, you might feel your heart fill with joy.

3   *A person you feel neutral about* or indifferent to, such as someone at the bank, the grocery store, or work—or a neighbor you've never met before. This person needn't arouse any particular feeling in you.

4   *A difficult person* or someone whom you find to be challenging, such as a grumpy colleague or frustrating friend. When you try to send kindness to the person, it may seem a little daunting. You may feel overwhelmed by the idea and think, "How can I wish her well after what she did?" This practice isn't about becoming a doormat or allowing someone to abuse you; holding on to deep resentment, however, can take a toll on you physically and emotionally.

Often, resentment hurts you much more than it does the other person, who may have long since vanished from your life. If this difficult person is still in your life, this practice can give you the opportunity to practice loving-kindness in action. Sending kindness to the difficult person will help you begin to release the destructive habits of anger and hate.

5   Finally, you will send loving-kindness to *all living things*, including all people, animals, and plants. You don't have to stop at planet Earth, either; you can extend loving-kindness toward the entire universe.

Instructions for Formal Loving-Kindness Meditation

The following instructions will take you through the entire list above, starting with sending loving-kindness toward yourself and ending with directing it to all living things.

When you practice the formal loving-kindness meditation, try to spend about five minutes on each group: yourself, a loved one, a person you feel neutral about, a difficult person, and all living things.

If you find yourself falling asleep during your meditation, try experimenting: If your eyes are closed, open them. If the room is too hot, open a window. If it doesn't work to practice at night, try first thing in the morning. There is no right or wrong way to practice these meditations. Do what works best for you.

To begin this practice, take a comfortable position and close your eyes. A good position is sitting on a chair or meditation cushion with your spine straight. If for some reason you are unable to sit up, it's fine to lie down.

1. Take a few deep breaths. The breath plays an important role in meditation. When you bring your attention to the breath, it can anchor you in the present moment. You don't have to think about the breath or change the way you're breathing—just *feel* the breath.

   Breathing in, feel the expansion of your chest or abdomen. Breathing out, feel yourself relax. If you find you can't relax, try to visualize the tension flowing out of your body with each out-breath.

   Sit quietly and allow yourself to connect with feelings of kindness and friendliness; this is the feeling you get when a child takes your hand, when you see your best friend, or when your pet comes to greet you. One way to generate feelings of kindness or friendliness is to remember a time when you did something generous for someone, such as sending your mother a card just to tell her you love her.

Try to remember how it feels to be generous, to offer help or kindness to another. You may feel a sense of expansiveness in your chest or a feeling of joy or calm—feel it now as vividly as possible.

As you access feelings of kindness and friendliness in yourself, gently direct a set of phrases toward *yourself*. Look over the following phrases and see if they resonate with you. If they don't, then create your own.

May I be happy.

May I be healthy.

May I be peaceful.

May I be safe.

Repeat the phrases as if you're gently speaking to a friend. It's important to drop into the meaning and feeling behind the words. Let the words be your guide, keeping you on track and anchored in the practice. Every time you repeat and feel these phrases, you are training your mind in loving-kindness.

If you didn't feel kindness toward yourself, you haven't done anything wrong. Let yourself reflect on a wish to be happy and peaceful. If you still feel nothing, remember that old mind habits take time to change. This is an opportunity to practice patience toward yourself without judgment or guilt. You can always come back to yourself as often as you like.

2   After a period of time, let go of yourself as the focus and shift your attention to a *loved one*. For example, think of a family member, good friend, teacher, mentor, or someone who has treated you with kindness and generosity—someone who has inspired or enriched your life. This should be someone you care about deeply and to whom you can easily extend friendliness and kindness.

Using the phrases from the previous page or creating your own phrases, replace "I" with your loved one's name. Imagine her face as you say the phrases. Allow good wishes, kindness, and warm feelings in you to flow to this person, wishing her well wherever she is in the world.

May _____ *be happy.*

May _____ *be healthy.*

May _____ *be peaceful.*

May _____ *be safe.*

3   After this deep connection with your loved one, shift your attention to a person you feel *neutral* about. This is someone you do not know well; you may never have spoken to him. Your gift of wishing kindness is anonymous and offered freely, requiring only your attention and willingness to wish a stranger well.

May _____ *be happy.*

May _____ *be healthy.*

May _____ *be peaceful.*

May _____ *be safe.*

4   After a period of reflection on a neutral person, let him go and shift your focus to a *difficult person*. This is someone

you may be in conflict with, someone you judge or resent. Start with someone who is annoying—but not the most upsetting person in your life.

May _____ *be happy.*

May _____ *be healthy.*

May _____ *be peaceful.*

May _____ *be safe.*

If opening your heart to someone you don't like seems too challenging, simply return your attention to yourself, sending and receiving your kindness.

5   Next, shift your attention to the *rest of the world*, to all people, animals, plants, the earth, and all living things. Think of people in other countries: children, women, men, leaders of the world. Think of your pets, animals in zoos, animals in shelters, and all that roam free. Think of your favorite places—the rain forest, lakes, rivers, mountains, oceans—or your favorite trees and plants.

May all beings be happy.

May all beings be healthy.

May all beings be peaceful.

May all beings be safe.

As you extend the feelings of friendship, caring, and kindness to all individuals and all forms of life, a sense of boundlessness may arise in you. Recognize and enjoy that feeling.

6   When you're ready to end your formal practice, bring your attention back to yourself. Take a few deep breaths. Gently begin to move your body. You might want to wiggle your fingers and toes.

If you have warm feelings inside, just rest with those for a moment. End your practice by opening your eyes and then, when you're ready, move out of your meditation position. Let the expansiveness and compassion you experienced during meditation follow you throughout your day.

Instructions for Informal Loving-Kindness Meditation

Loving-kindness meditation can be practiced informally. Everyday situations present you with many opportunities to shift old mental habits and learn to treat yourself and the world differently. In this book you'll learn how to send kindness to someone you notice at work, in a store, traveling in a car, bus, train, or plane.

You'll learn to direct kindness to yourself or others throughout your travels during the day: in the hospital, in doctors' or lawyers' offices, in meetings, waiting in checkout lines or at traffic lights.

And we'll explain how to send kindness to yourself if you're upset, cranky, or not operating at full capacity. You can also learn to send thoughts of compassion to people you're upset with, like your friend with the annoying habit that drives you nuts. You can use loving-kindness meditation when you can't sleep, are worried about something, or are feeling angry or fearful.

Repeating loving-kindness phrases in everyday situations is an invitation to connect with and strengthen feelings of kindness and friendliness. Here are examples of such phrases:

May everyone on this plane be safe.
May the person in the car next to me be at ease.
May all the people in this store be peaceful.
May I rest and feel relaxed.

Every time you repeat a phrase, you deepen the intention in your mind and heart for your own happiness and the happiness of others. You may begin to see that there's not so much separation between yourself and others. Everyone wishes to feel happiness—it is this wish for happiness that unites us all.

This practice allows you to open to the moment. Don't become attached to outcome; you are not trying to control things, but rather to learn to treat the moment with kindness. Just do the best you can and know that your best is good enough.

PART ONE

Loving-Kindness
Toward Yourself

Introduction

Loving-kindness is a wholehearted and genuine desire for the well-being of yourself and others. Loving-kindness meditation starts with yourself. Why is that? You practice this meditation for the purification of your own mind. If your mind is filled with blame and self-hate, it's hard to love yourself or anyone else.

As you practice loving-kindness you may begin to think and behave in a friendlier manner toward yourself. Meditation naturally teaches patience and tolerance. As you develop a friendlier and more caring attitude toward yourself, you'll begin to experience happiness.

How do you increase feelings of happiness? It starts with attention. As you begin to explore inner joy, you may find that you can make it grow. Try this: Bring to mind someone you like. Imagine him walking up to you, smiling, excited to see you.

What happens? Your friend's joy is infectious; you find yourself smiling, happy to see him. You don't have to think about feeling happy. You just feel happy.

Most of us don't pay much attention to the feelings of happiness. We tend to pay more attention to what is wrong. It's not uncommon to build relationships around problems, letting difficulties dominate the interactions. As you practice paying attention to your inner life, you'll develop a more positive, nurturing relationship with yourself.

Learn to Befriend Yourself

If you feel bad about yourself, your sense of self-worth may be low and your self-talk may be quite unfriendly, even mean. You may have thoughts that you're never good enough, that you're never going to meet your goals or have the life you've dreamed of. The negative voices in your head might sound like this: "I'm stupid and incompetent. I'm ugly and fat. Everyone else seems to have it together but me. Why did I do that? I'll never forgive myself. I'm a total failure."

Can you hear the unkindness in those words? Those are words you would never say to a friend you love and care about. Imagine what would happen if you looked at yourself, all parts of yourself—even the ones you don't like—with kindness and compassion. You might begin to see how some thoughts bring you pain while others bring you happiness.

Loving-kindness meditation can help change negative self-talk. When you befriend yourself, self-criticism and self-judging begin to decrease. As you practice compassion toward yourself, you'll find you can make friends with your inner critic.

Meeting self-hate with kindness can loosen its grip. Once you begin to free yourself, you start to respect and care for yourself as a good friend. In order for this to happen, you can't just read about loving-kindness meditation—you need to experience it. Actually practicing the meditation is key to removing the old habits. You begin to train your mind in kindness.

Discover Your Enormous Potential
for Happiness

Everyone wants to be happy. You may not realize that happiness comes from within you. Real self-worth is entirely internal. The exercises in this section will give you an opportunity to practice compassion and love for yourself. You may find that you'll experience feelings of joy and contentment—not just while you're doing the meditation exercises but long after your practice has ended.

The best way to start is to look through these different loving-kindness practices and see which ones resonate with you. Then do the ones you like. You can repeat the same one many times. Give yourself a chance to open your heart as you practice these meditations.

practices for

Loving-Kindness
Toward Yourself

Be Your Own Friend

The foundation of loving-kindness meditation is knowing how to be your own best friend. How do you treat your best friend? Is it with care, attention, love, and concern? Here is an exercise that offers you those same deep feelings of care and friendliness you show toward others. This practice helps you remember your core goodness and points you back to yourself.

1   Take a few deep breaths. Breathing in, feel the expansion of your chest and abdomen. Breathing out, feel yourself relax.

2   Remember times when you have felt open and friendly. It's the feeling you get when a child takes your hand, your dog comes running to greet you, or your sweetheart wraps you

in a warm embrace. The feeling is one of peace and deep contentment.

3   As these memories and feelings emerge, let yourself feel warm emotions. Now gently direct these phrases toward yourself:

May I be kind to myself.

May I rest in this moment.

May I be at ease.

May I be happy.

These words should not be expressed in a hurried or mechanical manner. Receive the meaning of these phrases as best you can. Let go of the outcome. Be very patient with yourself; remember you are practicing kindness.

Loving-Kindness Toward Your Body

Hate your thighs but love your eyes? Many of us would like to change some part of our body. Whether it's our height, weight, hair color, or teeth, most of us are dissatisfied with our bodies in some way. Why is this? We can point to TV ads, glamour and bodybuilding magazines, or being teased by our siblings.

Practicing loving-kindness toward your body means meeting each body part without judgment. Directing friendliness and acceptance to each part or region, allow your body to fully receive the gift of compassion.

1   Take a comfortable position and close your eyes.

2   Take a few deep breaths.

3   Visualize yourself feeling good about the parts of your body you really like. Rest in that feeling for a few moments.

4   Now focus on one part of your body you don't like. Treat this part of your body with kindness. Repeat these phrases:

May I be kind to my body.

May I make friends with my body.

May I be free from hate.

May I be free from fear.

5   Relax and let your breath comfort you. After several minutes, bring your attention back to the room.

Formal Peaceful Walking Meditation

Peaceful walking is a wonderful exercise, especially if you're feeling agitated or restless. It gives the body something to do while the mind calms down. It's also a way to point your mind toward loving-kindness for yourself. When you're practicing formal peaceful walking meditation, you're not trying to get anywhere. A walking path of ten or fifteen feet will do.

Walk anywhere you like: in your house, outside on a deck, on grass.

1 Stand still. Feel your feet on the floor or the ground.

2   Start walking very slowly. Keep your gaze focused in front of you.

3   Focus on the sensations in each foot as it touches the ground. There's nowhere to go, no other place you have to be.

4   When you arrive at the end of your path, stop. Slowly turn around and walk back to where you started.

5   After you have done the walking for a few minutes, begin to send these loving-kindness phrases to yourself:

May I be peaceful.

May I be free from worry.

May I be well.

May I be patient.

6   Allow yourself to find your own rhythm, and let the pace change with your needs. When you're ready, end the walk by sending yourself the loving-kindness phrases a final time, then go about your day.

Informal Peaceful Walking Meditation

Think of all the different circumstances that call on you to walk during the course of each day. You are walking from the time you get out of bed in the morning until you get back into bed at night. Every time you walk to your car, into a store, or around your neighborhood, it's an opportunity to practice informal peaceful walking meditation. This type of loving-kindness activity is very simple.

1   Walk at your normal pace.

2   Bring your attention to your body as you walk.

3   As you walk through your neighborhood, house, or shopping
    center, repeat these phrases to yourself:

    May I be well and happy.

    May no harm come to me.

    May I be carefree.

    May I smile and enjoy this moment.

Follow the Ocean Waves

If you're lucky enough to live near the ocean, the beach is a wonderful place to practice loving-kindness meditation.

1   Find a comfortable place to sit down and watch the waves.

2   As each wave starts to curl, say one of the loving-kindness phrases. So when the first wave that you see rolls in, say, "May I be happy." On the second one, say, "May I be healthy." On the third, "May I be peaceful." And on the fourth, "May I be safe."

3   Then start over and keep repeating the phrases to yourself. Sometimes the waves are slow to roll in; be patient and allow yourself to linger with the meaning of the words as you wait for the next wave. Remember to receive the meaning of the phrases and your good wishes for yourself.

Take Kindness for a Drive

Have you ever found yourself running late for work and trying to make up the time by driving too fast? Do you then end up getting angry at any driver who gets in your way? Anger is a powerful force that can overtake the mind. The moment you start to feel the pressure of running late, try this:

1　Take several deep breaths.

2　Use your breath as a reminder to pay attention to your body. You're not thinking about breathing—you are feeling the sensation of breathing. Shifting your attention to feeling your breath will help you drop below the agitation.

3   As you drop into your breathing, pay particular attention to your self-talk. Are you being mean or critical with yourself for being late?

4   As you breathe out, replace the mean words with the following phrases:

May the anger I feel at this moment leave me.

May my body be calm.

May my mind be peaceful.

May I be at ease in this moment.

Keep repeating the words to yourself. Let the breath and the words guide you into calmness.

Remember Kindness in Your Family

It takes great effort to raise a child. It's easy to remember all the things that your parents did wrong, but what about the things they did right? Take a moment to remember how kindness was expressed in your family.

1   Let yourself sit comfortably and bring your attention to your breath. Feel the air at the tip of your nose.

2   Think of your family. What do you remember about kindness in your family? Did your mom or dad cook your favorite food or make you a special birthday cake? Did your parents take you swimming or teach you how to ride a bike? Did you have a favorite aunt who liked to spoil you? A brother or

sister you liked to play games with? How were kindness and generosity expressed in your family?

3   Visualize the goodness coming from your family toward you. Let yourself feel this love and say to yourself, "May I feel the care and love I received as a child."

4   Rest in the feeling of being loved and cared for.

Beach Walk

The next time you find yourself on the beach, try this:

1   Walk at whatever pace is comfortable.

Say one or more of the phrases below, then repeat the pattern. Keep walking for as long as you like.

May I be filled with loving-kindness.

May I be well.

May I be carefree.

May I be peaceful.

2 Every once in a while, stop, look around at the color of the sky, listen to the sound of the waves and the wind, notice any sea birds. Let yourself receive your kind words. As you walk, simply pay attention to the beauty of the world around you as you repeat your loving-kindness phrases to yourself.

Forgive Yourself

Forgiveness is essential to letting go of self-hatred and self-judgment. When we forgive ourselves, we release deeply held negative feelings; it frees us from the past.

1   Take a comfortable position and close your eyes. Wherever your breath is most obvious to you, put your attention there. It might be at the tip of your nose, in the back of your throat, in your chest, or in your belly rising and falling.

2   Remember a situation for which you have not been able to forgive yourself.

3   With the same kindness you would extend to a dear friend, repeat this phrase yourself: "For any hurt I caused myself in this situation, knowingly or unknowingly, I offer myself forgiveness."

You may repeat this phrase as many times as you like. When you feel the gentle wave of kindness wash over you, allow yourself to float in this feeling of forgiveness.

4   If feelings of unworthiness come up, breathe gently, accept these feelings, and remember the goodness in your wish to forgive yourself.

5   When you feel ready, end this meditation. Open your eyes, wiggle your fingers and toes. Release any guilt you're holding or negative thoughts you have about yourself. Give yourself credit for doing an exercise that may have been difficult for you. Forgiveness can arise from the simple intention to be kinder to yourself, and it can soften the mental pain you may have suffered.

Melt the Ice

Try this the next time you can't stop thinking that you're a terrible person who hasn't contributed anything of worth to the world:

1   Sit comfortably in a quiet area. Let your scattered thoughts and energies begin to settle like dust to the ground. Notice any painful or uncomfortable thoughts vying for your attention. Let them arise and pass through your mind like clouds.

2   Now bring to mind someone from your past who loved you. Perhaps it was a grade school teacher who recognized you had a gift for language, or a mentor who helped you hone your skills as a carpenter.

3   Imagine this person is sitting in front of you, smiling at you. Feel this person extending love and care to you in the form of radiant light, like the rays from the sun.

4   Let your heart open up to receive this warm light. If your heart feels blocked, imagine this barrier as a thin layer of ice, melting to make room for this love.

5   As this love comes into you from this special person, feel your heart fill and then overflow with love and gratitude. Let this feeling flow throughout your entire body, filling you with the sensation of peace and ease.

6   Breathe calmly for a few minutes. End by returning your attention to the world around you. Now carry this feeling out into the world.

Love Travels Like the Wind

Gandhi referred to love as the "subtlest force in the universe," because, like the wind, it can travel anywhere. Love is a deep feeling of goodwill that actually has the power to make you and others feel happy.

What would it be like if you were to meet anger with love? What a miracle that would be! It takes strength to choose to love wholeheartedly in the face of anger. It may be a lifelong challenge, but it's certainly worth the effort. So the next time someone acts out in anger toward you—a colleague lashes out at work or the bus driver rolls his eyes because you used all pennies to pay your fare—see if you can send love his way instead of anger. Anger dries your heart out; love moistens it. Think to yourself, "You give me your anger. I do not accept it. Your anger is still your own."

Direct these loving-kindness phrases to this person in your mind:

May you be filled with loving-kindness.

May you be peaceful and at ease.

May you be happy.

The greatest happiness you could ever hope for would be to have a loving heart in any and every situation. It might be tough to be compassionate at times, but it's certainly worth it.

Find a Safe Harbor

It's important to feel safe and protected. We've all experienced unpleasant, distressing events that have left us feeling unsafe, as if we're in harm's way. As you begin to bring more attention to feelings of security and protection, you might discover that it's easier to access a sense of safety than you thought.

1   Take a comfortable position and close your eyes.

2   Take a few deep breaths. Breathing in, feel the expansion of your chest and abdomen. Breathing out, feel yourself relax. With every breath you can feel yourself getting more and more relaxed. Rest in this feeling of relaxation.

3   Visualize yourself in a place—real or imagined—where you feel safe. Notice all the details: where this sanctuary is, what it looks like, what you look like, and how you feel.

4   Now let the feelings of being safe and protected wash over your body, mind, and heart as you repeat the following phrases over and over like a song:

May I be safe.

May I be at ease.

May I be at peace.

May I rest in the feelings of safety.

After about ten minutes, end this meditation by opening your eyes. Wiggle your fingers and toes. This is a practice you can use if you want to experience more moments of security in your life; it's a practice you can turn to when you don't feel safe.

Love on the Go

Love allows you to see the good inside of yourself. To love yourself is to accept the events in your daily life, good and bad. Through mindfulness you can wake up to your own goodness and befriend it. Then you can take it with you wherever you go.

Think of a time when you did something kind for someone or helped someone out. Let your mind fill with that memory of kindness. Remember how grateful that person was for your good deed. Perhaps you took the time to listen to someone's story. Simple acts of kindness can have a big impact on a person's life.

Rest in that memory of your kindness for a few minutes. Let yourself feel again what it was like to have helped someone in need. This is not stroking your ego—recalling this memory and resting in these warm feelings allows you to tap into your own goodness.

Give Yourself a Present

When was the last time someone gave you an unexpected gift? Maybe your partner brought you flowers on a Monday, or a friend sent you an effusive letter. Remember how this unexpected gift made your heart swell. The truth is, we can offer gifts of kindness to ourselves any time. The next time your spirits need a boost, try this exercise:

1   Breathing in and out from the area around your solar plexus, your chest area or "heart center," begin by feeling kindness toward yourself.

2   Breathe past any blocks to this kindness, past any feelings of unworthiness or frustration with yourself. Then drop beneath that place and find a spot where you can feel the kind of care for yourself that you would feel for a small child or wounded animal.

3   Following your breath, say or think these phrases to yourself:

May I be filled with loving-kindness.

May I be healthy and strong.

May I feel calm and at ease.

May I be happy.

Repeat these phrases over and over. When you lose focus, come back to the phrases and say each one slowly, as if you were unwrapping a gift to yourself.

Notice Your Small Acts of Kindness

Have you ever noticed that you spend a lot of time focusing on the things you do wrong? What if you began to notice the small acts of kindness you do for others every day? Focusing on the positive things you do can help you feel more connected to the world around you.

1   Sit in a comfortable position and close your eyes.

2   Think of something that you've done or said that was kind or generous—perhaps you offered to watch your friend's kids so she could go on a date with her partner, or you comforted a friend when she was feeling blue.

3   Let yourself feel any sensations of happiness that accompany these memories of offering kind acts to others. Let yourself feel the goodness of doing things for others.

4   When you're ready, open your eyes, wiggle your toes, and head back out into the world with a stronger sense of your inner goodness.

Count On Support

Think of the last thing you did that scared you to death. Maybe it was kayaking the Grand Canyon, or competing in a triathlon, or simply speaking before a crowd. Chances are that if you took on any challenge, you likely had at least one person supporting you. Either it was someone who ran the river with you or a friend to whom you were able to recount your public speaking nightmare. Being able to count on someone for support can help diminish the fear involved.

The next time you take on a challenge, be sure to tell a friend or ask them to accompany you. In the words of Everett Ruess, a young explorer of the American West in the 1930s, "A true companion halves the misery and doubles the joys."

Learning to find support through tough times is one small way of being kind toward yourself.

May You Be Happy

If it seems strange to feel love or affection for yourself—maybe you've been told that this makes you selfish and egocentric—then you can practice by wishing the same pure affection for yourself that you might feel for yourself as a little baby.

1   Sit comfortably and bring your awareness to your breath. Feel it rise and fall like the waves on the ocean, moving in and out of your chest and belly in a smooth, continuous wave.

2   Picture yourself as a small child. Visualize the feel of your own smooth skin, your small hands, toes, and rounded belly.

3   See yourself encircled in the warm, glowing light of the sun, a breeze blowing over your skin.

4   Holding this image in your mind, say to this small child—to yourself—"May you be happy." See yourself smiling, receiving these well wishes and receiving the sunlight, the cool breeze. See yourself at ease. Repeat this phrase until you can feel this warmth and affection in your own body.

5   When you're ready, bring your attention back to the world around you. Carry this affection that you felt for yourself as a small child around with you throughout the day.

Let the Light In

The next time you're feeling agitated or frustrated, try this simple meditation to help you breathe more fully, drop into your body, and notice the magnificence of the world.

1   Let your mind quiet down. Let go of any thoughts of planning or the future. Notice this moment—the sounds, the air temperature, the chair that supports you. Linger in this moment and let it come to life.

2   Breathe steadily in and out, letting any fears or feelings of discomfort leave your body with each exhale. On the inhale, let light enter your chest cavity and fill you with ease. Notice

just how good it can feel to simply sit, breathe, and drink in the moment.

3   Bring your attention to your heart area. Let a radiant light emanate from the center of this area, and feel a softening in your heart. Let this light fall over your whole body, from your head down to your chest, torso, hips, thighs, knees, calves, and toes. Feel yourself shrouded in this light.

4   When you're ready, gently recite these phrases to yourself:

May I be filled with loving-kindness.

May I feel healthy and strong.

May I feel calm and at ease.

May I be happy.

Remember that you can access this compassion toward yourself at any point in time. Kindness and ease are just a breath away.

Accept Yourself

Is there some part of yourself that you have trouble accepting? Maybe you've always struggled with your weight or are overly critical of your achievements. These feelings of inferiority can leave you feeling isolated and separate from the world. You can learn to accept—even learn to love—these parts of yourself.

1   Take a comfortable position and begin by directing loving-kindness toward yourself. You can repeat the four basic loving-kindness phrases or simply say, "May I be filled with loving-kindness." Let the phrase evoke the feeling within you. Feel your body relax.

2   When you're ready, choose one aspect of yourself that you
     have trouble accepting. Maybe you're terrible at making deci-
     sions or have a compulsive addiction to sugar.

3   As you bring to mind this part of yourself you don't like,
     begin to surround it in loving-kindness. Feel the warmth
     melt your feelings of aversion and dislike as you begin to
     accept this part of yourself. Say your loving-kindness phrases
     or try these:

May I accept this part of myself.

May I love myself just as I am.

Learning to accept difficult parts of yourself is a great way to
begin treating yourself with greater friendliness and compassion.

Clear Your Heart

We've all been hurt by someone. Many of us carry this hurt around with us for years, not realizing the cost to our well-being. Have you ever considered that carrying this anger, hurt, and resentment around is actually limiting your ability to live fully in the present? It's taking up space in your heart that could be used for loving. When we forgive another we release this weight and clear the heart for more joy.

1   Start by bringing to mind the past hurt that is causing you suffering. Perhaps someone did you wrong years ago and you've been harboring ill feelings toward this person all this time.

2   Now bring your attention to your breath. As you breathe, let yourself feel any emotions that arise, such as aversion, anger, or grief. Let these feelings arise and then dissipate like clouds in the sky.

3   Now focus your attention on your heart. Notice how not forgiving this person constricts your heart, as if a thick briar were growing over your heart and shutting out the light. Breathe into your heart as you state your intention: "I forgive you for the harm you may have caused, knowingly or unknowingly, out of fear, confusion, or pain. To the extent that I am able, I forgive you. I release you."

4   As you release this person, feel the weight lift off of you; feel the space in your heart clear out and make room for the light to shine in.

Find a Friend in You

Even if you disappoint yourself, that doesn't mean you have to stop being a friend to yourself. Would you berate a friend if her soufflé came out of the oven flat or she didn't meet her exercise goals for the week? Well, then, why would you do that to yourself? Try to see yourself as a friend would. With this loving-kindness meditation, you can learn to befriend yourself even when you disappoint yourself.

1   Breathe in and out from your solar plexus—your chest area, your "heart center." Breathe as if all of your experiences were coming from your heart.

2   Notice any blockages or resistance you might feel about
     directing kindness toward yourself. Now drop below these
     feelings and come to rest in a place where you can care for
     yourself, accept yourself, and wish kindness toward yourself.
     Say these phrases to yourself:

May I accept myself just as I am.

May I show myself the same kindness I would show to a loved one.

May I be free from pain and suffering.

May I be happy.

Loving-kindness meditation helps you develop compassion—for yourself, for others, and for the dark emotions within you. Loving-kindness helps you cultivate self-love.

Tap into the Force of Kindness

One way to experience more gratitude for life is to count your blessings. This can be hard, especially when you're struggling. But remember, even when you're struggling, there's a force of kindness surrounding you; you just need to learn how to tap into it. This practice will help you refocus your attention on the world of good that surrounds you at all times.

1   Sit in a comfortable position, bring your attention to your breath, and think of things that you're happy about. Maybe you have an adorable niece whose smile brightens your day or a dear friend who gets you out for walks. Maybe your friend

sends you creative text messages that read like poems. Make a mental list of all the things you're grateful for.

2   Let yourself feel this gratitude in your body. Maybe it makes your heart feel lighter or causes a smile to creep onto your face. Feel the weight of your burden lift as you keep making an inventory of all you have to be grateful for. If your mind wanders, come back to your breath and continue your gratitude list.

3   Now say these phrases to yourself:

May I cherish the gifts offered to me.

May I be peaceful and at ease.

Notice how focusing on the things you have to be grateful for diminishes your suffering and reminds you how truly blessed you are.

Kindness Is a Choice

You could steer your mind toward aversion, unkindness, or anger—this possibility is before us every single day. But you can also make the choice to act with great friendliness and compassion by setting your inner compass toward loving-kindness. So if your mother-in-law barks that you're late when you arrived right when she told you to, or someone steals the parking spot you've been relentlessly searching for, remember that you have an inner compass and it's set toward compassion and kindness.

Even if you instinctively accuse your mother-in-law of misinforming you or you angrily flip off the parking space thief, you can always reset your compass and let it guide you toward your goal: kindness.

It starts with awareness. You become aware that your desired object is loving-kindness.

1   Say to yourself, "May I be filled with loving-kindness." Let the words invoke the feeling in your heart. Feel your heart grow and expand with this feeling.

2   Whenever you are pulled by anger, by the impulse to lash out at someone who does you wrong, simply repeat this phrase to yourself: "May I be filled with loving-kindness."

3   Positive intentions have a powerful and directive quality in our lives. If we try to do the right thing, we are essentially guiding our ship in a positive direction.

Breathe in Joy

This practice will help you access the joy hidden within you.

1   To begin this meditation, concentrate on the beating of your heart. You can place your hand on your heart if it helps you focus. If at any point you find your mind wandering, bring your attention back to that beating rhythm.

2   Now imagine that your breath is flowing in and out through your heart.

3   As you picture breathing through your heart, call up any experience that made you feel really good. Maybe it was basking in the warm glow of your birthday candles or climbing an apple tree in the heat of summer. Let a feeling of gratitude

fill your heart as you reexperience this moment. If you can't feel anything, just focus on the beating of your heart as you breathe in and out.

4   With each in-breath, you bring this feeling of joy into your heart, and with each out-breath you send this feeling out to others.

5   Continue breathing in joy and breathing out well-being for others.

6   Before you end the practice, find a way to anchor these feelings or call them to mind in the future. Maybe there's a word you can use to remind you of these feelings. Or perhaps simply placing your hand on your chest will bring them to mind.

7   When you're ready, gently move your body and return your attention to the world around you.

Things That Make You Feel Good

Cultivating positive emotions can prepare us for the hard times to come. By finding more ways to let happiness in, we strengthen our heart muscle and find that when tough times come, as they inevitably will, we can deal with them more skillfully.

Spend some time thinking about the things that make you truly happy. Make a mental list or write these activities down. Not only can you experience joy in this moment by just thinking of these things, you can also go out and do them!

The next time you're down in the dumps or dealing with a particularly challenging situation, you can call on the strength you developed from doing things that make you feel good. Here are some ideas to get you started:

- Riding your bike to the ocean
- Writing while listening to music
- Drinking a cup of hot tea
- Sleeping in
- Eating a nourishing breakfast
- Taking a bath before bed
- Burning a candle on a cold winter night

Calm in the Face of Change

A wise person once said, "The only thing in life that doesn't change is change itself." Life is a constant cycle of beginnings and endings: Your grandmother dies and your best friend announces she's pregnant. You're promoted at work and your mother retires after thirty years of service. You go through a breakup and your brother celebrates his marriage.

Life is not static. It's a constant opportunity to love and let go. In each moment we can let go of the old and welcome in the new. Rather than clinging to the past, we can release ourselves to the force of life and know that we're part of a never-ending cycle of change.

The next time some big change stares you in the face, breathe easy, knowing that it, too, will change. You can say to yourself, "May I be calm in the face of change in my life."

PART TWO

Loving-Kindness Toward Difficult Emotions

Introduction

The meditation practices in this section invite you to meet difficult emotions in yourself from a perspective of kindness and compassion, and to discover the deep stillness within you that underlies turbulent emotions. At times, your life may feel like the surface of the ocean on a stormy day—subject to high winds, rough seas, and major swells.

Deep down, however, the ocean is undisturbed. When you begin to practice loving-kindness meditation, you begin to get in touch with your own deep stillness—a place of profound peacefulness that lies below the surface.

The waves of our own emotions can show up in many ways. They can gently roll in, or they can be like a tsunami. They can pass without notice, or they can come crashing in and toss you around like a piece of driftwood. Everyone is challenged by emotions. Sometimes anxiety, anger, and depression can sound like the roar of the ocean in your mind. No one wants to drown in these dark emotions.

What relationship do you have with your stormy emotions? How do you ride those waves? Some emotions we recognize immediately. For example, getting angry may be old hat to you; the slightest thing might provoke you to fits of rage. Or maybe, like millions of others, you're more prone to paralyzing anxiety, unwilling to take action for fear of unknown consequences. Or maybe you carry around feelings of shame, regret, and grief for past actions.

How do your treat yourself when these dark emotions rise up in you? Are you mean and critical of yourself for having these feelings? Or do you accept them as part of life? This section will help you learn to ride the waves of your turbulent emotions with greater ease, style, and grace.

It's important to learn to pay attention to difficult feelings when they arise. Such emotions can affect your health and your relationships. It has been well-documented that stress affects the body, contributing to everything from high blood pressure to heart problems.

Relationships can be profoundly affected by uneasy emotions, sometimes causing you to lash out or stew in judgment about the perceived shortcomings of others. Loving-kindness meditation invites you meet your difficult emotions with kindness instead of defensiveness, judgment, anger, or fear.

Kindness and Compassion

Practicing loving-kindness is an easy way to tap into the peacefulness that lies just below the surface of your ocean of emotions. As we explained in part one, one way to practice loving-kindness is to repeat a loving-kindness phrase that has meaning to you, a phrase that generates compassion. Or you may want to visualize a time when you felt great friendliness for yourself or others.

Another technique is to reflect on your positive qualities, including your generosity. The repetition of words, visualizations, or reflections can help trigger feelings of kindness and compassion for yourself and others. Use all of these strategies or the one that works best for you.

When you practice loving-kindness toward difficult emotions, allow yourself to take on an attitude of curiosity as you simply pay attention, without judgment, to what arises in you. If you continue to be unkind toward yourself or others, let yourself be accepting of your reaction. If you feel sad or tearful, know that it is not an uncommon experience. Before you can change a feeling, you must first acknowledge it.

As you practice these meditations, use your breath to anchor you in the present moment. It's in the present moment that you can move from despair to hope. Then gently face the difficult emotions with kindness, just as you would gently care for a good friend going through a rough time. Imagine offering your anger a comfortable place to sit or your grief a cup of tea.

It's a radical idea, but try it and see what happens. In this section you'll learn to meet whatever emotions arise in you with kindness and compassion.

The following practices will help you ride your difficult emotions more easily. Mindfully using loving-kindness meditation can help change your relationship with such feelings. It is possible, even with all of life's pain and fear, to find inner freedom and joy. It's easier than you think.

practices for

Loving-Kindness Toward
Difficult Emotions

Befriend the Difficult

It's easy to let negative self-talk tempt you to plunge into your dark emotions. Feeling helpless and afraid can become all consuming. But you can learn to trust yourself and your capacity to stay present and open. When you stop reacting and begin to soften to your painful emotions, you can transform your relationship with the difficult. Whenever you find yourself feeling bad, try this:

1   Take a comfortable position. Bring your attention to your breath, and feel it in your body. Pay close attention to where you first feel your breath entering and exiting your body; maybe it's at the tip of your nose, or perhaps you feel the air

flowing down the back of your throat. Let the sensation of your breath anchor you in the present moment.

2   Now say these words to yourself:

Let me be free of worry.

Let me be free of pain.

Let me be free of fear.

Let me be free of anger.

3   Allow the feelings that these gentle words evoke to soothe your difficult emotions. Take time to feel the meaning of the words and see your body relaxing, the tension in your shoulders and jaw releasing. As you practice making friends with your painful emotions, have faith in your capacity and ability to befriend them.

Be Still

If you're restless and don't know what to do with yourself, stay where you are. Just be still, be quiet. Let the eagerness to do something cool down. Let the pull of the outside world release its grip on you. Just as the sediment in a bottle settles to the bottom, so will your emotions if you let them be still.

1   Wherever you are in this moment, stay there. Don't go anywhere. You are right where you need to be.

2   Bring your attention to your breath. Take three or four deep breaths. When you inhale, let it be deep. When you exhale, let the breath out slowly.

3   Now repeat the following phrases to yourself a few times. Every time you say the words, let them penetrate your restlessness.

May I have courage.

May I trust myself.

May I have patience.

May I be free from fear.

Remember, you are right where you need to be.

Don't Look Back

The past is over, the future has not come yet, and we only have the present moment. Do we really want to spend this moment going over the same old story? Haven't we run through this scene a hundred times? Don't we know all the players and all the lines by heart? Of course we do, but we get caught up in it anyway. It's a habit. Our inner life can be like that, old stories that just keep rolling on.

1 A very easy way to work with mind habits is to check in with your body. In this moment what is your body telling you? Check to see if you have tight muscles anywhere. Be sure to check your jaw, neck, shoulders, lower back, and belly.

2   Now check to see how you are breathing. Is your breath shallow, fast, slow? Are you sighing?

3   Take a deep breath and let it out slowly. See if you can let the rhythm of your breath become gentle and even. As you repeat each one of these phrases, let yourself receive the meaning of the words:

May I be free of anger.

May my body relax.

May I be free of worry.

May I be at ease in this moment.

As soon as you bring your attention to the present moment, unhappiness and struggles can dissolve.

Accept the Task

What can you do when life feels overwhelming? No one can do your emotional work for you. You have to go deep inside yourself and find your own answers.

When you feel overwhelmed by your life and your ability to meet its challenges, turn toward loving-kindness. Try meeting your feelings of being overwhelmed with kindness, friendliness, and compassion. Let your kindness roll over you like a gentle wave.

1   Take a comfortable position. Notice if you're holding any tension in your head, shoulders, back, or belly.

2   Bring your attention to your breath. Breathe at your own rhythm—you don't have to change anything. Just breathe naturally. Feel your breath as it travels in and out of your body.

3   Think of someone you really care about. This could be your best friend or a child. Rest in the warm and tender feelings you have for this person.

4   Now repeat these phrases as you greet yourself with the same warm feelings you generated for this beloved person:

    May I be free of my fear.

    May I have courage.

    May I experience great success.

    May I accept the challenge of this task.

5   Let yourself rest in the glow of your own kind feelings toward yourself. You can repeat these phrases any time you feel overwhelmed.

Stop the Struggle

Are you so busy getting everything done that you no longer enjoy what you're doing? Are you starting to resent the job you once were excited about? If you feel you're being pulled in too many directions, you probably are.

Check in with your self-talk. Do you sound miserable? Are you feeling like a victim? If so, it may be time for a change—not necessarily in what you are doing but in how you are doing it. Don't let your mind go wandering off like an untrained puppy—keep bringing it back.

1   Find a comfortable place where you can relax, uninterrupted, for a few minutes. Using your breath as an anchor, breathe in and out at your own rhythm. Don't try to force anything. Take a deep breath and let it out slowly. Do this three or four times.

2   Close your eyes. Imagine yourself relaxed in your favorite place.

3   Now repeat these phrases:

    Let me be at ease.

    Let me be free from worry.

    Let me overcome my difficulties.

    Let me be peaceful.

4   When your time is up, open your eyes. Slowly start to move your body. A gentle stretch may feel good. As you go about your day, repeat those phrases as often as you can. Learn to rest in the ease and comfort that the loving-kindness phrases offer.

Write a New Story

The next time something upsetting happens, ask yourself, "Have I felt this before?" Situations change, emotions change, but the stories we tell ourselves about past situations and emotions can stick with us. The story can be filled with fear and worry. Next time you are stuck in an old story, try this:

1   Find a comfortable place to sit undisturbed for a while. Shut out distractions. Turn off your phone and shut the door if you can.

2   Take a few deep breaths. Feel where you are holding tension in your body. Check your jaw, shoulders, back, and belly. Use your breath to help you relax. See the tension leaving your body as you exhale.

3   Try to be as kind to yourself as you can in this moment. Even if you feel the old hurt feelings sinking their teeth into you, keep renewing your intention to bring kindness to yourself.

4   Now repeat these phrases to yourself over and over like a song:

Let me be free from the past.

Let me be free from worry.

Let me be free from fear.

Let me feel peace.

Take a Fear Break

When your mind gets caught in an eddy of fear—thoughts of how scary the world is, how meaningless your life feels, how little you've accomplished—it's time to take a fear break. Fear doesn't have to be the guiding force in your life.

1   Sit quietly and begin to pay mindful attention to your breathing. Take a moment to notice what's going on in your body. Are your muscles rigid, is your heart constricted, or is your brow furrowed? Let the tension melt away with each breath.

2   Now take one of those fear thoughts and place it in your heart. Let your heart open wide to take in this fear. See your

heart—red, pulsating, and warm—as it absorbs this fear and transforms it. As you hold fear in your heart, say these words to yourself:

May I meet fear with courage and an open heart.

May the force of love transform my fears.

May I be happy just as I am.

Fear arises when you feel separate from the world around you. As your sense of separation diminishes, fear will lose its grip on you. There is a stronger force at work within you and that's the force of love, which brings with it feelings of appreciation, generosity, caring, and patience.

Befriend the Monsters

Loving-kindness is a heart meditation that's meant to be taken off the mat, or meditation cushion, and out into your relationships, work, and the streets of your city or town. It's about developing a friendly attitude toward yourself and others.

Over time, the repetition of the phrases and the practice of the meditation will blend and become your actual experience; you will actually begin to feel loving-kindness radiating from within you out into the world.

A very simple way to practice great friendliness toward—and acceptance of—yourself, including your dark emotions, is to call upon your loving-kindness phrases any time you feel impatient, frustrated, or judgmental with yourself. Try these phrases:

May I be held in compassion.

May I be free from pain and sorrow.

May I be at peace.

If you're feeling frustrated with someone else, direct the loving-kindness phrases toward this person. Let the phrases emerge from your heart, like a bird taking flight:

May you be held in compassion.

May you be free from pain and sorrow.

May you be at peace.

Through this practice you can begin to learn caring acceptance of both joy and suffering—your own and that of others.

Let Your Shadow Walk
in Front of You

Is there something you've done that you feel ashamed of? Perhaps it's an old pattern of behavior that keeps cropping up and sabotaging your success right when you're feeling your strongest.

1   Begin by saying, "May I accept all aspects of who I am, the dark and the light."

2   Imagine your shadow self coming to the surface, into the light.

3   Let your shadow walk in front of you, in full view.

4   Again, say to yourself, "May I accept all aspects of who I am, dark and light."

More Joy, Please

How can we make room in our hearts for more joy? It depends on what emotions are living there now. If you open your heart, you might see that fear, resentment, pain, grief, and unfulfilled longing are cluttering up that space. How can joy exist in a place like this? If you want to make your heart a hospitable place, begin sweeping, clearing, decluttering. You have to make more space in your heart for joy to enter.

1 Try imagining your fears, worries, and pains as objects that you can tie to a red balloon. Grab ahold of the string, pick the fear up off of your heart, and tie a nice, secure knot. Now let go of the balloon and feel the weight of your fear lifting

off of your heart. It may be stuck in places, so you might have to nudge it along. Remind yourself that you're making more room and it's okay to let the fears go. Do this with each constricting feeling that's taking up space in your heart.

2   As you tie each of your constricting emotions to the end of the balloon, repeat these loving-kindness phrases:

May I be free and at ease.

May I open my heart to peace and joy.

May I trust that I am safe.

3   Feel the space that is created in your heart. Let the joy come fill that space.

Raw Beauty

There's a certain comfort in knowing we can face life just as it is—no artificially induced highs, no special protections from things going "wrong," just life in all of its raw beauty, challenge, pain, and joy. The next time you find yourself trying to control the uncontrollable, do this instead:

1   Set your intention for this practice—for example, "May this practice help me open to the world as it is, no matter what is happening."

2   When you feel yourself closing down to pain or unwanted experiences, try instead to open your heart to the experiences no matter what is happening. Let an expansive, all-embracing

feeling take root in your heart and open your arms to the pain or discomfort—just as you would open your arms to a young child running toward you in glee.

3   Notice that embracing difficulty with loving arms helps transform the experience. Say to yourself, "I accept all aspects of my experience."

Let the Clouds Pass Over

Have you ever noticed that the sky isn't harmed by the clouds that pass by? Whether the day is gray and bleak, or bright blue with wispy tendrils of clouds, the sky remains unchanged. We can learn to be this way with our own feelings. No matter what's going on outside of us, through the cultivation of awareness and mindfulness of the moment we can establish a place within ourselves that is stable, unchanging. The next time the world outside of you throws you for a loop, try this exercise:

1   Take a moment to notice your breathing. Let your chest rise and fall with each breath.

2   Say to yourself, "May I find a place of stability and stillness within myself."

Stay focused on your intention to find stability and calm in a changing world.

Meet Anger with Kindness

As strange as it may seem, loving-kindness can be particularly effective in anger-provoking situations. By learning to soften toward others, you can learn to meet anger with kindness.

1 Bring to mind a situation where someone acted out in anger. Maybe it was a coworker who told your boss that you'd done a sloppy job on your last project. Notice any feelings that this brings up in you.

2 Do you want to lash out at her? Do you feel the urge to remind her of all of her faults and all of the ways she's let the company down in the past? Let these feelings arise and, like clouds in the sky of your emotions, let them pass.

3   Find a place within yourself where you can remember that meeting anger with anger only creates more anger. You can say to yourself, "You offer me your anger. I don't accept it. The anger still belongs to you."

4   Feel the anger coming toward you and let it slide off, like water over your skin. Let it pool around your feet and evaporate with the heat of the sun.

If you meet anger with kindness, the kindness gives the anger no avenue to travel down, and anger is then left lost and alone, wandering the streets looking for a vessel in which to lodge itself. Don't let yourself be that vessel.

Awaken the Goodness Within You

Many of us secretly carry around the distorted notion that we're flawed, defective, or not enough. Self-compassion is a radical act that allows you to soften toward yourself, leading you to the discovery of your own innate goodness. The following practice will help you access the deep reservoirs of happiness within you:

1   Begin by taking a comfortable, seated position.

2   Focus your attention on your solar plexus in your chest, in your "heart center." Breathe in and out, and anchor your awareness in the sensations emanating from this area.

3   Breathing in and out from your heart center, say these phrases
    to yourself:

    May I be peaceful and at ease.

    May I be joyful.

    May I be free from physical pain.

4   Any time you feel your attention wander, gently return to
    the sensations in your heart center and your loving-kindness
    phrases. Let the words help you experience kind feelings
    toward yourself. Notice any potential blocks toward this self-
    kindness, such as thoughts like "I haven't done anything to
    deserve kindness"—and then let them go.

5   After a few minutes, you can end by slowly moving your body
    and returning your attention to the world around you.

By softening to ourselves we can learn to recognize the good that
rests within us, just waiting to be awakened.

A Day of Heartfulness

Your heart is a muscle. It needs to be exercised. If your life experiences lead you to lock your heart up and throw away the key, then your heart may be out of shape. If that's the case, you may need to practice living from your heartful, rather than fearful, mind.

Have you ever noticed that some people live from the heart? Some people are just naturally trusting and loving, and appear to believe in the goodness of the world. But what if you live your life on the lookout for danger, ready to protect yourself from hostile forces. Do you want to be guided by fear—or love?

The bravest thing you could ever do is to love. What would it be like to respond from your heart rather than from your fear-filled head? You would begin to see that your world contains more allies than you could ever have imagined. When we open our hearts, our world begins to expand.

Try acting from your heart for a day—try a day of heartfulness. Like you would with a day of mindfulness, you drop into your heart and respond to the world as if your heart were guiding you. See if you can feel your heart open as you repeat these loving-kindness phrases throughout the day:

May I listen to my heart.

May I respond to the world from a place of love.

May I know that I am safe and protected.

May I know deep, trusting love.

Drop the Weight

Do you carry the weight of your pain and sorrow with you wherever you go? Old sorrows can feel like a heavy burden, blocking your access to joy and appreciation for life. When you're ready to let go of that weight, try this exercise:

1   Bring to mind an old hurt that's been living inside you. Perhaps it's the pain of a broken heart, of a lover who betrayed you.

2   Allow yourself to notice the feelings this hurt brings up in you. Do you feel aversion? Do you want to shrink away from it and close your heart? Allow these feelings to simply arise in you. Don't judge them or push them away.

3   Behind the hurt, you might also notice feelings of sadness or grief. Let yourself feel compassion for this part of yourself that was hurt by the other person. Feel your body relax as you let go and soften into these feelings.

4   With your mindful awareness, extend kindness toward yourself. See yourself wrapped in a warm, protective blanket of kindness, protected from harm. Say these phrases to yourself:

May I live free from suffering.

May I have the strength to forgive those who have caused me harm.

May I be happy.

By forgiving ourselves, we are able to miraculously go back in time and rescue a part of ourselves we left behind. The past begins to lose its grip on us as we become more whole.

Bow to Your Anger

How do you greet the emotions of anger, grief, fear, and disappointment within you? Do you treat them with meanness, self-judgment, and anger—or with kindness and compassion? Do you tell yourself you shouldn't have these feelings?

The challenge is to greet your own dark emotions with the same care and compassion you would the pain of someone you love. The next time your mind plays tricks on you, telling you what a miserable person you are, try this:

1   Take a deep breath and notice the thoughts your mind is sending you. Are they filled with self-recrimination? Let the thoughts arise and see them pass before your mind's eye.

2   Acknowledge these feelings and thank them for coming. You can even name the feelings, saying, "Thank you, fear, for coming. Thank you, sadness. Thank you, anger, for letting me know you're here." You can even imagine respectfully bowing to your dark emotions.

3   Be patient and kind toward yourself. Greet your feelings and sensations with a spirit of great friendliness. Soften your heart toward your own shortcomings.

You don't have to let your emotions control your life. If you can learn to acknowledge them, experience them, and then let them go, they won't have such a strong grip on you.

Balance Your Emotions

The world is filled with magic and it's also filled with pain. With this practice, you can cultivate a stability within yourself that allows you to accept sadness and not just cling to joy.

1   Find a comfortable position, close your eyes, and begin to breathe in and out from your solar plexus, your chest area, your "heart center." Breathe as if all of your experiences were coming from your heart.

2   Let a good feeling into your heart. To find this feeling, think of someone you love dearly or a place where you felt totally safe and protected. Let this feeling permeate your whole body.

3　Now think of an event that made you sad, like a fight with your best friend. Let this feeling of sadness wash over you. Don't try to control it or change it. Just let it be. Notice what this sadness feels like in your body.

4　Now let both of these feelings—the love and the sadness—pass in and out of your heart like waves. Don't grasp onto one or push the other away. Just let them rise and fall like waves. Continue in this way until you feel a calm balance between the feelings of love and sadness.

5　When you're ready, take a deep breath, open your eyes, and move around.

This practice teaches us how to find balance in the midst of our chaotic, ever-changing emotions.

Break Old Habits

It's hard to accept ourselves and the world just as we are, to not react to pain by closing down our hearts. It can be hard to break the habits of unkindness, aggression, and hatred. But you can start with this simple practice. The next time you're given the opportunity to react to the world through nonconstructive means such as anger or aggression, try sending loving-kindness phrases instead. The words will help bring up positive feelings and replace old habits. Say these words to yourself:

May I be held in compassion.

May I be free from pain and sorrow.

May I be at peace.

And to those who challenge you to abandon your heart and choose anger, send them kindness instead:

May you be held in compassion.

May you be free from pain and sorrow.

May you be at peace.

Spark Your Happiness

Why is it that when we see another person glowing with happiness—perhaps a friend just realized a lifelong dream of getting a book published, or another friend finally got to take a vacation in Hawaii—we feel a little twinge of envy rather than being genuinely happy for that person? Why is it that we think our own happiness is diminished by the happiness of others?

Perhaps deep down we think there's not enough joy to go around. Well, here's the breaking news: Happiness isn't a limited commodity. In fact, happiness grows happiness. Your bliss sparks the same in others.

So, if your friend's tropical vacation reminds you that you need to take a vacation yourself, or her published book reminds you of the work you still need to do on your own book, let yourself feel the envy within you, and then let yourself rejoice in her happiness, knowing that your happiness isn't diminished by her accomplishment. Say to yourself, "May your joy spark the joy of others."

There's enough happiness to go around. We all have access to a deep well of happiness within.

Only Boring People Get Bored

A teacher once said, "Only boring people get bored." One way to counteract boredom is to practice loving-kindness, which increases our sense of joy, wonder, and appreciation of the world. The next time you feel dull and lifeless, try this exercise:

1   Close your eyes, take a deep breath, and feel your body relax. Follow the rhythm of your breath.

2   When you're ready, open your eyes and look around you. Notice the breeze rustling the leaves of the plum tree outside your window. See how the light through the window brightens the room. If you have houseplants, look at how their leaves grow toward the light. Take a moment to notice all

the man-made objects in the room—the computer and its tangle of cords, the chair you're sitting on, the mug with your steeping tea.

3   Follow your breath as you take in your surroundings. Now say these phrases to yourself:

May I increase my appreciation of the world around me.

May I be conscious of the complexity and wonder of the world.

May I be fulfilled and at peace.

4   Notice how just shifting your awareness and appreciating your surroundings can lift you out of a mind-set of boredom and into a world of wonder. Paying attention to the little things in life eliminates boredom because it gives your mind something to appreciate.

Open the Box of Love

No matter what you've lived through, no matter how scary or peaceful your life has been, no matter what harm you've caused others or others have caused you, you are still intrinsically whole. We are all complete and connected to one another.

Showing loving-kindness means embracing all parts of ourselves and the world around us. Through practice, we stop denying different, "unlikable" parts of our experience. The goal is to accept what comes into our lives, and accept what leaves our lives without fear, desire, or aversion.

You can learn to access this natural goodness within you and others simply by doing a formal or informal loving-kindness meditation. By repeating loving-kindness phrases, you can access this loveliness, this perfection that rests within all of us. Our original goodness is like a gift just waiting to be opened. Let the loving-kindness mantras be the force that pulls open the bows on the box.

Let the light in by saying these phrases to yourself:

May we be filled with loving-kindness.

May we be healthy and strong.

May we feel calm and at ease.

May we be happy.

When the Cheese Drives You Nuts

The absence of loving-kindness is a cue to slow down and pay attention to what is happening inside. After all, loving-kindness is most valuable when you're having a hard time being kind to others.

The next time you find yourself irritated at the well-dressed French tourist in front of you in line buying dozens of exotic cheeses when all you want is your sandwich—and now—take a breath and notice how you're feeling in your body. Is this person really irritating, or are your emotions out of whack? Take another deep breath and notice any sensations in your body. Is your breathing labored? Is your heart racing? Are you tired?

Take a moment to treat yourself with kindness and you may notice that the French lady is not only no longer irritating but, in fact, you love her shoes enough to tell her so—and the huge smile that erupts on her face changes your whole afternoon.

The next time you notice that an innocent stranger is bugging you, take a moment to check in with yourself and offer yourself a little kindness. Repeat the following phrases until you start to feel their effect:

Just as I wish to be happy, all beings wish to be happy.

May I be peaceful and at ease.

May I be free from suffering.

Balance on the Waves

Finding balance may at times feel like a struggle. Life is filled with extremes, some painful and others pleasurable. You might be grieving over the death of your beloved grandmother—and a few days later be surrounded by family and friends as you celebrate your birthday. How can we hold these two extremes without shutting down?

The Buddha said the greatest happiness is to know peace that is unchanged by changing conditions. With this inner stability, you can ride the waves of contrasting emotions and experiences without losing your balance.

The next time you're overwhelmed by the contrast of joy and pain in your life, say these phrases to yourself:

May I ride the waves of pleasure and pain with ease.

May I be peaceful and at ease.

It's possible to experience happiness in the midst of pain and sorrow. It's possible to be happy and sad at the same time. This is part of the balance of life, and practicing acceptance of this pleasure-and-pain dynamic helps us let go of our need to control our experiences. Accepting this duality is the birthplace of balance.

Monster Mind

When we were kids, fear came in the form of monsters in the closet or under the bed. When we're adults, the monsters are "fear thoughts" hidden in the dark recesses of our minds. We fear so much—losing our partner, a job, money, or our health.

The more you begin to notice and name fear thoughts, the less impact they have on your life. The next time you find yourself overcome by fear, try simply naming it. For example, let's say you're walking home from work one day and you start making a mental inventory of all the terrible things in your life: "My back kind of hurts. Maybe I need surgery. I don't think my insurance would cover that. What if I lose my job?" You can stop these fear monsters—or at least impede their progress—by simply naming each one of these thoughts "fear."

As you practice this strategy, you'll begin to see that the thoughts don't scare you quite as much. You'll see that thoughts are just thoughts and you don't have to follow them into the wild jungles of your mind. The next time you notice the fear monster, name it and say these words to yourself:

May I be free from fear.

May I be calm and at ease.

May I be at peace.

Even if your mind and heart are filled with fear, loving-kindness can pierce through. Through this practice you can learn to recognize and acknowledge the fear—or anger or judgment—without getting caught up in it.

When the Party Is Over

Do you ever catch yourself clinging desperately to happiness? Say you're at a party that you've been looking forward to for months, and now people are starting to gather their jackets to go, at which point you feel yourself wanting to grasp the moment so it won't end. You don't want to leave the party. Perhaps you feel that happiness is fleeting and once this moment is over, it's back to your dull life.

At the root of this clinging is fear: fear that there won't be other good moments to come. The next time you catch yourself tenaciously holding onto a happy moment, try this:

1   Stop and bring mindful awareness to the moment. Notice
     your heartbeat, the flow of your breath in and out of your
     body.

2   Say to yourself, "May the happiness I feel in this moment be
     unending."

Remember that true happiness isn't dependent on outside events.
Happiness is a quality that lives deep within you—one that you can
call upon and cultivate by letting go of and accepting each moment
as it is, without a sense of clinging, knowing happiness will soon be
back again.

PART THREE

Loving-Kindness
Toward Others

Introduction

Part three explores how you can use loving-kindness meditation with family, friends, acquaintances, and people you find challenging to deal with. When you practice loving-kindness toward the people in your life, you're actively wishing for their happiness and well-being.

Think about your own life. Think of the times when others have offered you kindness and what that has meant to you. Remember a time of great difficulty when you allowed a friend or loved one to help you. When we come to understand the pain and sorrow—and joy—of others, we take a step toward being more connected, loving, and intimate with our world. It's through our kindness and capacity to be intimate with one another that we can begin to heal the pain and suffering in the world.

As human beings we all have the capacity to be kind and compassionate toward others. Many of us don't often think about kindness, but reflecting on the times when you've been thoughtful to another person enables you to see that you've already practiced loving-kindness naturally.

Offering Kindness

Offering kindness can be as simple as saying "thank you" to the people you love. Taking the time to listen deeply to your partner is also such a gift. It's easy to allow the rush toward the next moment to rob you of the opportunity to practice kindness in the present, yet one simple act like this can shape your entire day.

You can also send kindness to those people in your life who trigger negative reactions in you. Maybe it's a coworker who needs to be the center of attention, or a friend you perceive to be self-absorbed. If you learn to send love rather than judgment in these moments, you take a step toward greater harmony, both within yourself and in your relationships with others.

The Art of Giving

Practicing the art of giving can also be a way to cultivate kindness. The notion of giving certainly doesn't have to imply giving *things*. It might well mean the giving of your time or your talents. In this busy world it can be a gift to simply spend time with another.

Learning to Forgive

Forgiving the people in your life whom you find challenging can be an act of kindness. One way to do that is to focus on their good qualities. We all have positive and negative qualities. When we're practicing loving-kindness, we are looking for the good.

But being kind doesn't mean letting people take advantage of you; forgiveness is about your inner life and shifting how you feel. That means dropping any resentment you have about the other person.

It's possible to offer forgiveness even if the other person doesn't change or doesn't accept your forgiveness. It's not about him—it's about what's going on inside of you. What keeps you hostage from your own kindness?

As you practice loving-kindness meditation toward others, you begin to see a number of ways compassion can be offered. Kindness can become a habit if you keep bringing your attention to it.

How do you show kindness to people you don't really know but you see often? For example, how do you treat the boy who bags your groceries, the teller at the bank, or the waitress or busboy in your favorite restaurant? Try a friendly word or a warm smile. When you acknowledge someone with an open heart, you often get back more then you give.

Kindness toward others is really very simple, and these next exercises are designed to help you practice it and to send good wishes and happiness to the people in your life. When you become aware of how a simple act of emotional generosity has the power to deeply touch someone's heart, you develop an appreciation for how such an act is filled with tremendous dignity and integrity.

practices for

Loving-Kindness
Toward Others

Behold the Mystery

Birth is a mystery. When a baby is born, everyone is reminded of the preciousness of life. It's easy for the heart to open to—and love—this tiny, wrapped-up bundle of joy. Next time you hold a small child, feel the loving-kindness you have for him. Notice the smile on your face as you look at this tiny wonder, and listen to your sweet words as you speak to him. When you think of this child, send these words of loving-kindness:

May you live a long and happy life.

May no harm come to you.

May you sleep with ease.

May you always know you are loved.

Friendship Power

A best friend is always glad to see you. A best friend is easy to be with, and you know that if you need her she'll be there for you. She listens to your life stories; you can tell her any of your secrets; and she share your dreams for happiness. It's easy to send a best friend loving-kindness. Here's an opportunity to wish her well:

1   Picture your best friend in her favorite place. Where would that be? What does it look like?

2   Imagine a time when you were together to talk, laugh, or cry. Remember how good it felt to be together.

3   Allow the warm feelings you have for this person to fill you. Let yourself rest in the good feelings you have for your friend.

4   Repeat these phrases as you visualize your best friend:

May my best friend be healthy.

May my best friend be free from worry.

May my best friend be peaceful.

May my best friend be carefree.

We Are Family

As we get older, we tend to drift from our biological families. Your parents, who fed, housed, and nurtured you for so many years, now have their own lives to lead. Your brothers and sisters, with whom you may have shared a room and competed for attention, likely have families of their own at this point. But through loving-kindness meditation, you can bridge the distance by generating love in your heart and sending it out toward your mother, father, sister, or brother.

1   Bring to mind a beloved family member. See his face, eyes, smile.

2   Now focus on some special quality that you love about this person. Maybe your brother has a great sense of humor or your mom makes the best tomato bisque this side of the Mississippi.

3   Feel your heart overflow with joy and with love for this person. Let him rest in your heart, free from harm, whole, happy.

4   Now send that feeling of love out toward this person through these phrases:

May your days be filled with joy.

May you be peaceful and at ease.

May you be happy.

Loving-kindness practice brings us closer to those we love when it isn't possible to hop on a plane to go see them.

Be Kind to Your Neighbors

Do you have a neighbor who has picked up your newspaper, collected your mail, watered your lawn, or watched your pet? Here is a way to wish your neighbor well:

1   Sit in a comfortable position.

2   Take a moment to bring your attention to your breath.

3   Now reflect on how your neighbor has helped you out. Notice that his kind actions kept you from worrying about your house or your pet while you were gone.

4   Visualize your neighbor. Let yourself feel gratitude for having such a good person in your life.

5   The next time you find yourself thinking about your neighbor, let your appreciation, your warmth, and your respect for this person flow out of you toward him. Say to yourself, "May my neighbor's life be filled with peace and ease."

Wish Them Well

Think of the people in your life for whom you feel mostly indifference. These are people you see at work, in the grocery store, at the gym, in yoga class, in a restaurant. Imagine sending them your kind wishes. You might see them often, but you don't have any real connection to them. Let yourself appreciate and respect them for their good deeds, remembering that everyone has done something good in their life.

1   Take a comfortable position.

2   Bring your attention to your breath. As you inhale, feel the expansion of your chest and abdomen; as you exhale, feel yourself relax.

3   Now call to mind a person whom you consider an acquaintance. As you reflect on this person, simply wish her well.

May good things come to you.

May you be healthy.

May you be free from pain.

May you be safe.

You can repeat just one of these phrases or make up your own. The intention is to wish this person well, remembering that, just like you, she carries inside of her an innate goodness and wish for happiness.

Appreciate the Challenger

Think of someone you don't like, someone who bothers you. If more than one person comes to mind, just focus on one at a time. It's easy to want the difficult person to just go away; since you can't wish that into reality, however, here's something you *can* do:

1   Find a comfortable place to sit and relax. Turn off your phone and turn away from your computer screen.

2   Bring your attention to your breath, inhale deeply, and exhale slowly. See the tension leaving your body as you exhale.

3   As you bring your difficult person to mind, think of all the good things that he has ever done or said. Yes, we are looking

at the good in this person. Allow yourself time to reflect on his goodness.

4   Appreciate that person for any of his kind actions, even if you were not actually present for them.

5   Repeat these phrases and send them to your difficult person.

May your good deeds support you.

May you be calm.

May you be free from anger.

May you be well.

Let your heart of compassion open to this individual as you practice feeling the oneness that connects us all.

Thank You, Teacher

Teachers show up in our lives in many different ways. They are not always found in classrooms—sometimes they're our own children or friends, and sometimes they cross our paths for just a short time. Think of someone who has been a teacher for you: a person who has freely given you the gift of her wisdom and has made a difference in your life.

1   Find a comfortable place where you can sit and reflect on this wise person.

2   Think about your breath and take a few moments to feel it travel in and out of your body. Notice your inhale. Notice your exhale. Let the rhythm of your breath help relax you.

3   Reflect on your teacher. Feel a sense of well-being and con-
     tentment for all that she has taught you.

4   As you experience these good feelings about your teacher,
     direct these well wishes toward her:

May my teacher be healthy.

May my teacher be happy and peaceful.

May my teacher be safe.

May the wisdom of my teacher be passed on to many.

When you're ready to stop, let yourself smile at the thought of
your teacher. Any time you think of this person, it's an opportunity
to wish her well.

Share Your Happiness

At times we block ourselves from facing the suffering in the world because we're afraid it will ruin our own happiness. The last time you walked past a homeless person on the street—bedraggled, cold, and hungry—did you avert your eyes for fear that her suffering might creep under your skin and steal your own sense of great fortune? This attitude can lead to a sense of isolation and transitory happiness.

The next time you find yourself trying to block out the world's suffering in order to protect your own sense of happiness, try this loving-kindness phrase. Let it emerge from your heart like a bird taking flight: "May the happiness I feel permeate all of my actions and be shared with all beings."

Loving-kindness allows us to see ourselves in others, to see that we're all connected.

A Friend in Need

Wₑ can learn to cultivate deep feelings of love and appreciation for life and then extend those feelings toward someone in need.

1   On the in-breath, visualize your beating heart. See it in your mind: vital, life-giving blood pumping through it and enlivening your entire body.

2   Now bring to mind someone you care for deeply. Maybe it's a young child whom you've watched grow over the years. See her walking toward you, her arms outstretched, a big smile on her face. Let her smile light the fire of love in your heart. Imagine opening your arms to her and taking her into your

embrace. Feel the warmth of this embrace course through your body.

3   Let the warmth radiate off of you like the rays of the sun toward the earth.

4   Now send this warm heart-love out to someone you know who is in need right now. Maybe someone who has just recovered from surgery or is dealing with a chronic health condition. Imagine this circle—you, the child, the one in need—and let the warmth of this love-fire pass around and around among you.

5   When you're ready, end by returning your attention to the world around you.

Random Acts of Gratitude

In the practice of *naikan*, or introspection, you reflect upon what you receive, what you give, and the harm you may have caused other people. You do this to develop a sense of appreciation for others. Try the next practice as a daily reflection. Write the answers down or say them to yourself.

What have I received today? Notice the little things you receive all the time but perhaps take for granted. For example:

- My partner made the bed this morning.

- My company provided us with scones, cheese, and fruit at our meeting this morning.

What have I given others today? Think of the acts of kindness, big and small, that you've extended to others today. For example:

- I called my mom to check in.
- I sent a note to a friend I haven't heard from in a long time.

What troubles and difficulties have I caused today? Notice the impact your actions can have on others. For example:

- I was short with my partner when she called today.
- I took the last seat on the bus this morning, meaning others had to stand.

This practice can help you stop asking what gifts others owe you and begin asking what gifts you can give to others.

Open the Door to Your Heart

Loving-kindness helps us open rather than close our hearts to others; it teaches us to respond with kindness where we may habitually respond with anger or frustration. Loving-kindness is both a practice and a habit. If you want to break the habits of judgment, resentment, and envy, let this practice help you open the doorway of your heart.

It's easiest to practice unconditional love by thinking of someone you care about, but eventually you will be able to extend this love to all beings, regardless of whether or not you know, love, or even care about them.

1   Call to mind someone you care about. It could be someone in your family, a dear friend, or a child who's shot his love arrow into your heart and made you his captive.

2   See this person in your mind. You can say his name to yourself. Once you have a sense of his presence, direct loving-kindness phrases toward him:

May you be filled with kindness.

May you be safe and protected from harm.

May you feel joy.

Notice how bringing to mind someone you love fills your heart with joy and brings a smile to your face. By opening your heart to those you already love, you're practicing opening your heart to all beings.

The Wishing Well

The next time you're feeling agitated—say you're stuck in traffic or caught waiting in a long line at the grocery store—try this exercise. It can help you feel more connected to the world around you, making your agitation melt away.

1   Bring your awareness to your breathing. Feel your lungs fill with air on each inhale and relax with each exhale.

2   Now let a feeling of warmth enter your heart center. Breathe in and out of this area as if you were experiencing the whole of the world from there.

3   Now concentrate on someone near you, or visualize this person in your mind's eye. It could be the stranger walking past you on the street or the person in front of you at the checkout stand.

4   See this person surrounded in light. Imagine the small details of her life. She gets up each morning, showers, eats breakfast, battles traffic—just like you do.

5   Let yourself feel affection for this stranger. Each of us goes through a thousand little battles each day just to survive.

6   With this person in mind, silently say, "May you be well." Let the warmth and light in your heart center radiate toward this person, as if you were wrapping her in sunshine.

7   Notice how this practice makes you feel. Do you feel just a little more compassion for others in the world?

Friendship to Spare

Cultivate the practice of giving. We can be generous with our kindness and with our time. Generosity can mean smiling at a stranger, opening the door for someone whose hands are full, or truly listening to a friend. The simple act of being truly present with others is the greatest gift we can give them.

1   The next time a friend comes to visit, focus your attention on her. Don't worry about what else you have to do that day or anything that came before that moment. Just be present and take the moments as they come.

2   Take the time to look directly into her eyes. See her. To help you appreciate this person, remember that one of the

great blessings in life is friendship. Good friends fill us with love, are concerned for us when we're struggling, listen to us when we're confused, and share in our joys. In addition, good friends can strengthen our own positive qualities. So, one prescription for becoming a wiser and more caring person is to spend time with wise and caring friends.

3   And as your appreciation for this friend begins to well up in you, silently repeat these loving-kindness phrases for her:

May you be filled with loving-kindness.

May you be healthy and strong.

May you feel calm and at ease.

May you know peace.

4   See if simply saying these phrases to yourself when you listen to your friend connects you with your heart and your love for her.

Your Mother's Kindness

No matter what happened later, our lives started out with a singular act of kindness: Our mother allowed us to live in her body, nourishing us with her blood and enduring tremendous pain to bring us into the world. No matter how you feel about your mother now, this act alone is worthy of a lifetime of gratitude.

1   Sit comfortably and bring your awareness to your breath. Feel it rise and fall like the waves on the ocean, moving in and out of your chest and belly in a smooth, continuous rhythm.

2   Now bring your mother to mind. Imagine her as she may have been when she was pregnant with you. Imagine her

cradling her belly—cradling you in her hands. Let a warm light emanate from your own heart center and surround your mother.

3   Continuing to encircle her in light, say these words softly:

May you be filled with loving-kindness.

May you be peaceful and at ease.

May you be happy.

4   Let the intention of these phrases fill your mind and course through your entire body. Let yourself feel genuine affection for your mother.

Close this practice by thanking your mother for the gift of bringing you into this world. No matter what came after, your existence is due in part to the selfless act of your mother carrying you in her own body.

See Your Father's Goodness

There are people in our lives who are challenging to deal with. For you, perhaps it's your father, whom you deem to be hotheaded. One way to foster a better relationship with people whom we find challenging is to focus on their goodness. This might seem strange. Why can't you just focus on all the things that drive you crazy about them?

By focusing on the positive, you can feel a greater connection to your father (or someone who's challenging), which can help you treat him more like a friend. For example, of your ornery father you might say:

- He is incredibly compassionate toward people in need.

- He is a wonderful listener.

- He's a great athlete.

If you focus on the negative, it's easy to feel hurt, angry, and resentful of all that people are not. If you focus on the positive, you can begin to address the negative traits with greater friendliness and compassion.

We All Make Mistakes

The next time you feel yourself getting annoyed with your upstairs neighbor for stomping around at all hours of the night, or becoming irritated with your best friend for being late again, try this practice to remind yourself that we're only human and we all make mistakes:

1   Sit in a comfortable position. Relax, quiet down any mental chatter, and direct your breathing and attention toward your heart. Let any feelings of irritation arise and gently flow out of you with each breath. Let a feeling of calm come over you.

2   When you're ready, recite some version of the following phrases. Let the words wash over your whole body and mind.

Just as I want to be happy, all beings want to be happy.

For any harm you may have caused, knowingly or unknowingly, out of fear, confusion, or pain, I forgive you.

When you're ready, return your attention to the world around you. Now go out and practice seeing others as human, fallible, and yearning for happiness, just like you.

Offering Kindness to a Friend

One way to nurture the feelings of loving-kindness is to welcome a dear friend into your heart.

1   Call to mind a good friend. You can say the person's name or draw an image of her in your mind.

2   Think of the things that you love about this friend, such as the following:

  •   She takes great pride in my accomplishments.

  •   She is reliable and spontaneous.

  •   Life is always more fun if she's there.

3   Let your feelings for this person blossom in your heart. See her smiling at you. See her surrounded in the light pulsing from your heart out toward her.

4   Now direct your loving-kindness phrases toward this person:

May you be filled with loving-kindness.

May you be healthy and strong.

May you feel calm and at ease.

May you be happy.

Let this practice allow you to extend to your cherished friend the same caring and kindness that you have for yourself.

Rays of Goodness

As much as you might like to think otherwise, even the most challenging people likely have at least one good quality. Learning to see the good in someone you find to be difficult can help you open your heart and feel less defensive and judgmental. That alone can transform your relationship with the person, even if she continues to test your patience.

1   Think of a person whom you find challenging. Maybe it's a friend who is so self-absorbed that she never asks how you are doing.

2   Now think of one good quality that you've noticed about this person. Maybe your friend is incredibly funny or attentive to her children's needs.

3   Notice that as you think of this person's good qualities, a spaciousness grows in your heart, a feeling of lightness overtakes you, and you begin to see her in a different light.

4   The next time you find it a challenge dealing with this person, simply say these words to yourself:

May my friend be happy.

May she be peaceful and at ease.

May she be well.

You can learn to extend kindness toward those who are difficult, even if their actions hurt you. By generating love and goodwill in your own heart, you begin to transform how you see those around you.

Meet Anger with Love

The goal of loving-kindness meditation is to have a river of compassion within you that is so deep and so wide that if someone were to pour his hostility into your river of compassion, it would just drown in your waters of kindness. If someone were to throw anger and resentment toward you, you'd be so immersed in compassion that the emotional outburst wouldn't cause a negative reaction in you.

The next time someone tries to toss his anger into your waters, simply say these phrases to yourself:

You give me your anger. I do not accept it. The anger still belongs to you.

May I respond to anger with kindness.

May the love within me nourish the souls of many.

The Generous Heart Gives

The easiest way to let go of attachment and fear is to be generous with others. When we cling to other people or things out of a sense of fear, we try to pull everything toward us so we can hoard it for ourselves The challenge of life isn't to see how much we can hold on to for ourselves, but to see just how giving we can be. So the next time you're feeling lonely and isolated, try doing something for someone else:

- Call a friend just to say hello.

- Make food for a couple with children.

- Write your mother a note of gratitude for her kindness to you.

- Pick a bouquet of flowers and bring it to the next dinner party you go to.

Generosity connects us to those around us. It breaks the illusion of isolation. Now go out into the world and give.

Envy No More

Can you feel truly happy for another person, or does her happiness bring on feelings of jealousy? Maybe your best friend's partner just proposed to her and gave her a ruby ring, while your partner continues to stall. Or another friend remodels her house while you're still renting. Do you truly share in this joy, or are you secretly envious, seeing it as a reminder of what's missing in your own life?

Sometimes we compare ourselves to others as a way of determining if we're successful, beautiful, or happy enough. We determine our sense of worth in relation to others.

You can learn to stop feeling threatened by the great fortune of others. The process begins by realizing that, just as you want to be happy, all beings want to be happy—and there's enough to go around. Your friend's happiness might remind you of a dream of your own, one that's buried within you waiting to emerge. Let her joy be a catalyst for your own dreams and desires. So, the next time someone you care about shares her joy with you, wish her well.

May your joy be unending.

May your happiness continue unabated.

The Mindful Minute

The real mindfulness practice is being present in your daily routine and actions. The goal is to cultivate mindfulness in any environment. You can learn to artfully create a spacious stillness in your mind, a radiant calm that allows you to be fully present as the world around you shifts and tilts.

As you walk through your day today, see if you can repeatedly return to the present moment. While you're working, can you bring your attention to your breath? If your body begins to ache, can you take a moment to stretch and breathe? As you're talking to others, can you remain aware of your own inner dialogue and quiet it down so you can truly hear the other people?

Start today and commit to twenty-four hours, one hour, or even a minute of mindfulness. Wherever you are right now, choose to pay attention, on purpose, to the world around you. When your attention begins to wander, say to yourself, "May I be calm and at ease. May I be peaceful." Don't try to fight or change your experience; just stay in the moment and see what comes.

You might be surprised to find that the more you're able to calm your inner chatter, the more your senses and awareness will come alive. You'll be able to see the world as it is, not as you think it should be. Not only will *you* benefit, but everyone in your life will benefit from your increased awareness and calm presence.

Let Kindness Steer Your Mind

Loving-kindness is a choice. It's a matter of what you do with your mind. Do you direct it toward anger and resentment, or toward love and concern for others? When you see a bus driver honking at a motorist blocking the bus lane on a busy street, you can either say, "Wake up, moron!" or you can remind yourself that the driver of the car is doing her best.

The next time you see someone make a mistake, remind yourself that we're all human.

You can even go a step further and wish others well—those making mistakes as well as those affected by those mistakes. To them all, say these words:

May you be safe and secure.

May you be free from pain and suffering.

May you be happy.

PART FOUR

Extending Loving-Kindness Toward the World

Introduction

Sometimes it's hard to know what to do when we see suffering on television or read about tragedies going on in the world. It's easy to want to ignore such terrible things, or to blame someone for them. You may believe that if you turn toward another's pain, you will be overwhelmed by his misfortune—and that's a very understandable reaction.

It's important for you to discover how much of someone else's pain you can endure and where to set boundaries in terms of protecting yourself emotionally in such situations. However, it's equally important to know you can set limits with others while still responding with kindness and compassion.

To be compassionate is to sense from within what it's like to experience another's pain and sorrow. Suppose a child dies in another country; the grief that the mother feels is no different than the grief you would feel if your own child were to die. We all experience life's suffering and pain.

Why bother to reach out to a stranger or get involved in things that don't concern you? We are beginning to see that with the modern global economy, events in other countries impact us all sooner or later. We're beginning to see that we are not isolated from the rest of the world. And, as a result, we're beginning to see that our actions do matter.

We don't need to wait for a disaster to hit to reach out and be kind to one another. You never know how an act of generosity, compassion, or forgiveness can impact someone and reverberate in the world. Our actions and intentions do make a difference. We have to trust that our kindness has power far beyond what we can imagine, and that seeds of compassion sown at home can have far-reaching impact in the world.

Simple Ways to Spread Kindness and Compassion

Every day presents opportunities to offer some small act of kindness. As different people come in and out of your life each day, look for ways to be deliberately kind. Your actions may start with a simple wish for someone's well-being: "May you find peace." If you see someone driving too fast, you could say, "May you be safe."

The process starts by breaking the habit of unkindness. It starts with consciously wishing someone well rather than reflexively responding with anger or frustration.

As you build your kindness muscle, your deeds of thoughtfulness may become more active: smiling and waving to a neighbor as you come home from work; acknowledging a coworker's efforts; listening to a friend without interrupting her; sending a card to a sick friend; welcoming a new neighbor with a plate of cookies or flowers from your garden.

You can also reach out to strangers by giving away used clothes or toys, or by making a donation to a local charity. You might volunteer to help children in need, offer some of your time at a homeless shelter, be a foster family for a rescued dog, or volunteer some hours helping out in an animal shelter.

You may also find that by practicing the formal and informal loving-kindness meditations in this book, you'll begin to look at the world in a new light. Rather than seeing greed and competition, you might see that we're all interrelated and dependent on one another. Your acts of kindness in words or deeds may not seem like much, but the rewards—both to yourself and the recipients of your kindness—are great.

Some days it will be easier than others to reach out with kindness. On days that it's difficult to do this—maybe you're tired or have been struggling at work or in your relationships—hold yourself in the arms of compassion and be patient.

As you begin to appreciate the value of compassion, you start to see others differently. You can appreciate that *all* humans experience joys and hardships—not just you—and you can see yourself interconnected with the world around you.

In this section you'll find a number of meditation exercises that will help you extend your loving heart of compassion out into the world. Start doing this in ways that are easy and natural for you, and remember that it's a wise person who knows his own limitations.

practices for

Extending
Loving-Kindness Toward
the World

It's Expensive to Get Sick

If you have good health insurance, it's easy not to give much thought to the people who don't. It's expensive to get sick! Bring your attention to the people who at this very moment are sick and not able to get the medical attention they need because they don't have—and can't receive—coverage. This practice will help you experience compassion for people you don't even know.

1   Take a few moments to sit quietly, relax your body, and be still. Let your breath be calm and steady. Breathe softly and use your awareness of your breath to anchor you in this moment.

2   Think about a stranger or loved one who is suffering and can't get medical attention. It's okay if you don't know this person. Let yourself feel compassion for how this person has to worry; let yourself experience her feelings of misfortune. Now, let your own good wishes to end her suffering come forward.

3   Silently offer your wish for her healing and well-being.

May you be free of your pain and worry.

May you find peace.

Open Your Heart to a Soldier

Who are the men and women who serve in our military? We may not know their names, but we see their faces on television and in magazines. Many are very young and far away from family and friends. Every day some of them risk their lives in order to do their jobs.

1   Take a few minutes to sit quietly and breathe softly. Feel your chest rise and fall with each breath. Use your awareness of the breath to keep you in the present moment.

2   Hold the image of a soldier in your heart and be aware of the feelings this brings up in you. Notice any sorrow, empathy,

or compassion that arises. Silently offer to a soldier your heartfelt wishes for her safety.

3   Direct the following compassionate phrases toward this soldier. Keep repeating them for a few minutes. See if you can feel your heart of compassion open as you wish this brave soul well.

May you be safe and out of harm's way.

May you return home and find inner peace.

It's also good to remember at this time the suffering of those who have loved ones serving in the military. They also need your heartfelt wishes of compassion.

May you find peace.

May you be free from worry.

Remember Your Goodness

It's easy to discount or forget the times when you have shown compassion to another. Perhaps you didn't even think about it as an act of compassion—you were simply aware of someone else's misfortune and you helped that person out. Whether your act of compassion was very simple or grand, you did reach out and lend a hand. This practice will help you remember and reconnect with such times:

1   Use your breath to bring you into the present moment. Feel your body breathing. Notice your chest rising and falling. Take a few deep breaths and feel your body relax.

2   Take a moment to recall some good deed you did. Recall what it felt like to reach out and lend a helping hand. Let yourself remember your feelings and rest in that memory.

3   Repeat these phrases to yourself a few times:

May my kind actions help me remember the good in myself.

May I remember my ability to help others.

4   When you feel ready, rest in silence and reflect on the memory of your good deeds.

Compassion Toward a Loved One

Bring to mind a loved one who is sick or grieving, or who is struggling with feelings of rejection or hurt. Picture his face, say his name, and be aware of your response. Let yourself feel your deep caring for this special person. Notice your heart opening to his pain and sorrow, and be aware of your natural wish to relieve his difficulty with your kindness and compassion.

1   Take a few deep breaths and let your body relax as you inhale and exhale.

2   Begin directing these phrases to your loved one:

May you be at peace.

May you be free from pain and sorrow.

May you be free from fear.

May you be held in compassion.

3   Remember that holding someone in your heart can be the greatest gift that you can offer.

Generosity in Your Town

Take a few minutes to think about where you live. It may be a big city or a small town—the size doesn't matter. It's home to you.

Think of all the people in the place you call home. What does it take to keep your town or city going? Call to mind the people who pick up your garbage, fix the roads, and keep the water running and the electricity flowing. Think of all the grocery stores, gas stations, and medical centers. Remember the fire fighters, police officers, emergency workers, schoolteachers, and bus drivers.

It's easy to take these people for granted. The next time you hear the garbage truck or fire engine sirens or you step onto a bus or buy eggs at the corner market, send loving-kindness to these workers, thanking them for their good work. Silently say these words to yourself:

May you be safe from harm.

May all the good work you do come back to support you.

Loving Creatures

If you have pets, it's very easy to feel kindness and compassion toward them. You know what it feels like to have your dog come running to you when you walk in the door, or to have your cat curl up on your lap when you sit down. But many creatures are not lucky enough to have someone like you as an owner; instead, they are abandoned or locked up in shelters. Let's send kindness to these unfortunate animals and pray for their well-being:

1   Take a moment to bring your attention to your breath. Feel
    the air coming in and out of your body as you inhale and
    exhale.

2   Think about a pet you have now or one you had in the past,
    maybe as a child. Remember the strong connection you had
    with this animal. Allow that feeing to expand to other crea-
    tures, such as birds, squirrels, rabbits, bees, and butterflies.
    Let yourself imagine any living creature at all and extend
    your kind wishes for its well-being.

3   Let your heart of compassion open to these animals—both
    those who are fortunate and those who are not—and wish
    them well. Rest and relax as you allow the joy that they bring
    you, or have brought you in the past, to fill your heart. Extend
    this joy to all animals in need.

Be Happy

Think about a celebration you attended for a good friend, maybe a wedding or birthday. The guests were nice, the food was delicious—especially the dessert—and your friend was particularly happy. Recall the good feelings you had in seeing your friend so jubilant. Feeling joy over someone else's good fortune is a practice in itself. It's the letting go of any jealousy, criticism, or comparison, and just taking delight in the happiness of another.

Take a few minutes to think of a good friend and focus on a situation in her life that is the source of happiness. Take delight in her joy and repeat these phrases:

May your good fortune never end.

May your happiness support you.

Look for opportunities to wish people well as you hear of their good fortune. Feeling joy for another's life situation is a way to deepen our loving-kindness practice.

People Watching

Have you ever noticed people's weight or how they're dressed and started to judge them? Do you ever make up a story about why they look a certain way, and then have an inner dialogue about what they should do to change? The things you conclude may be totally off base; the reality is you have no idea what's really going on in other people's lives.

The next time you start imagining negative things about a stranger, see if you can replace such ideas with kind thoughts, such as these:

May the world be kind to you.

May you be peaceful.

May you be free of your burdens.

May you know happiness.

Travel in Kindness

Travel can be difficult these days—with delays, large crowds, security, and tiny airline seats. But it's not the ticket agent's fault if your flight is delayed. And you can't blame the flight attendant if your plane sits on the tarmac for hours.

Every travel difficulty and inconvenience is an opportunity to practice either anger or kindness. After you arrive at your destination, you may continue to have challenges—perhaps with a car rental or reservations at your hotel. Here are some phrases to practice in an effort to both make your trip easier and replace frustration with kindness:

May I be peaceful.

May I be free from anger.

May all the people I have to deal with be at ease.

May we all be safe.

Stranger or Friend?

Loving-kindness is a meditation of tenderness, friendship, and concern for others. The great thing about loving-kindness is it doesn't depend on how other people feel about you. They might hate you or love you, they might be your best friends, or they may have no idea who you are.

This practice will help you experience loving-kindness for someone you barely know.

1   Find a comfortable position. Focus your breathing on your heart center in your upper chest. Feel your heart beating. Feel it soften like a muscle relaxing. Let the tension fall out of your face.

2   Now let a feeling of warmth enter your heart center. Breathe in and out of that area as if you were experiencing the whole of the world from your heart.

3   Bring to mind a stranger. It could be the woman who served you wine at the restaurant last night or the bagger at the grocery store.

4   Let the warmth and light in your heart center radiate toward this person, as if you were wrapping her in sunshine.

5   Say to yourself, "May you be peaceful and at ease. May you be happy." See this person smiling and receiving your gift.

Wishing a sense of well-being to people we don't know can help us break down the emotional barriers that create the illusion of being separate from others.

Plant Love

Maybe you find it impossible to care for anything other than yourself. Maybe thoughts of babies and puppies actually make you queasy. If so, there's still hope. Let's try extending kindness toward a plant!

1. Go to a nursery or store that sells houseplants.

2. Find a small plant that calls to you. Maybe you like the shape of its leaves, the color of the stems, the flowers on its branches.

3. Bring the plant home and set it in a spot where you'll notice it each day. Add water and care and you're good to go.

Research has shown that caring for something like a plant can lead to greater health and longevity. It can also help you feel more connected to your world.

If you're not quite ready to befriend a homeless person or are too afraid to smile at a stranger, practice loving-kindness with a plant. They don't talk back—and they certainly aren't as messy as a baby.

See the Good

Perhaps there's someone in your life you really find challenging to deal with. Maybe it's your mother-in-law, who only seems to complain. Maybe it's a coworker who can't seem to say anything positive about your projects.

One way to grow our compassion for others is to recognize that every single person alive suffers. It has been said that there are no heartless people, just heartless actions. So the next time someone does or says something that triggers you toward anger, try this:

1   Say to yourself, "Every one of us suffers. May this person feel calm and at ease. May she be happy."

2   Then, if you know a little about the difficulties this person has, list those in your mind:

- She is in great pain from the terrible migraines she gets.

- She doesn't sleep well at night from the pain in her knee.

- Her beloved father died when she was a teenager.

Seeing the good doesn't excuse the bad, but it helps put it in context. If we can see that others suffer just as we do, we can begin to cultivate the smallest seed of compassion for the pain they live with and can think of them with greater kindness. And eventually, we may be able to relate to them with greater compassion no matter how they treat us.

Forgive Those Who Have Trespassed Against You

Behind the harmful actions of others is a person in pain—someone whose beauty has been eclipsed by inner turmoil.

1   Bring to mind someone who has harmed you. Perhaps it's a past girlfriend who betrayed your trust.

2   Now say to yourself, "Just as I wish that others would forgive me for any harm I have caused them, I wish to forgive those who have harmed me, that we may cultivate a kind and loving relationship here in the present."

3   The phrases are meant to arouse the feeling of loving-kindness in you. Once the feeling arises, switch from a phrase to noticing the sensations of the feelings. If you lose sight of the sensations, switch back to a phrase, repeating to yourself, "Just as I wish that others would forgive me for any harm I have caused them, I wish to forgive those who have harmed me, that we may cultivate a kind and loving relationship here in the present."

It is the feelings of loving-kindness that will eventually help transform how we act in the world.

Open Your Heart Like a Flower to the Sun

Compassion opens our heart like a flower responding to the light of the sun. We can learn to recollect what love feels like and direct it to where it's needed most.

1   Sit in a comfortable position. Close your eyes and focus on your heart center in your chest. Breathe in and out from this area, as if you were breathing from your heart itself. Anchor your awareness in your heart center. Let all thoughts, feelings, and sensations arise from, and abide in, this center. Let light shine from this area out into the world.

2   Now think of someone who's in pain. Perhaps it's a friend who just broke up with her partner, or your sister-in-law who was recently diagnosed with an autoimmune disease.

3   Let the radiant light from your heart shine on this person. Allow the light to wrap itself around her life like a blanket enveloping a small child.

4   Say to yourself, "May this radiant light hold you and protect you through hard times. May you be filled with loving-kindness. May you be at ease."

Do No Harm

Why does loving-kindness matter? What's the point? Well, here's one: It can help us live in such a way that we don't harm others. What more could one human hope for than to live a life that doesn't intentionally bring harm to another? Let this practice help you cultivate a nonharming attitude:

1   Sit comfortably, breathing in and out through your nose. Feel your belly fill with air.

2   On the inhale say, "May my actions harm no one."

3   On the exhale say, "May my actions bring only good."

You can do this practice out in the world, repeating these phrases to yourself as you move through your day.

May We Be at Ease

Just as you want to be happy and at ease, so, too, do all those you encounter on any given day. The next time you're out in the world, try this exercise:

1   On your in-breath say to yourself, "May I be at ease."

2   On your out-breath say to yourself, "May all beings be at ease."

By stating this intention, you take one small step toward experiencing how intricately connected we all are. The words help establish the attitude. Your life isn't as separate anymore from that of the stranger on the street, because you now know that you're united by your shared desire to be at ease in the world.

Your Brother on the Street

If you live in a city or big town, chances are you see people suffering every day. Perhaps each morning as you rush to catch the bus to work, you pass a homeless man covered in tattered blankets, sleeping on the sidewalk behind a garbage bin. Maybe there's a man standing on the corner begging you for food or money.

It can be hard to know what to do. Do we stop and offer a sandwich or a couple of dollars every time we see someone in need?

One simple way to begin transforming your relationship with the suffering of others is to simply wish them well. The next time you see a person living on the street and don't know what to do, try sending him loving-kindness.

May you be free from danger.

May you find shelter.

May you receive nourishment, kindness, and the care that you deserve.

Can you feel a genuine sense of caring for the well-being of another? Loving-kindness can teach you to have the same goodwill toward a stranger in need as you do for a good friend. It can bring out feelings of love, tenderness, and warmth as you soften your heart and erase the emotional barriers preventing you from caring about the suffering of others.

Cultivate the Garden of Your Mind

Loving-kindness meditation lets you cultivate the garden of your mind, where you can plant seeds of kindness that will grow into flowers and plants and trees of generosity, which will nourish you and fill your life with great beauty and joy.

1   For this practice, simply find a comfortable position. Visualize a garden in your mind.

2   See yourself entering this garden and planting seeds in the freshly turned soil.

3   As you plant each seed, repeat the phrase, "May the seeds of kindness that I am planting today fill the world with beauty and joy."

4   See the seeds growing into beautiful flowers and plants, and bearing fruit. Your work is to give the seeds healthy soil to grow in.

5   When you're ready, end this practice.

Remember that you have a choice about what you allow to grow in the garden of your mind. Don't let the weeds of judgment, hatred, fear, and anger become so overgrown that they strangle the roots of kindness within you.

Get on the Kind Bus

The fact is, many people who help you don't have kindness on their minds. The bus driver who picks you up on the corner doesn't have your happiness in mind; he's just doing his job. The bank teller who hands you your receipt doesn't necessarily intend to display an act of kindness.

But regardless of their intention, everyone who contributes in any way toward your happiness and well-being is deserving of your kindness. Rather than focus on the motivation for their actions, focus on the practical benefits you receive.

You can learn to see that anyone who contributes to your happiness or well-being deserves your respect. The next time you're out in the world and someone helps you—either intentionally or not—silently say these words to yourself:

May you be filled with loving-kindness.

May you be healthy and strong.

May you feel calm and at ease.

May you be happy.

Imagine this person surrounded in a warm, healing, and radiant light. Imagine him amidst his family, vibrant and alive. Seeing the spark of humanity in others can help you grow kindness in your own heart and plant those seeds in the world.

An End to Suffering

Do you find yourself feeling overwhelmed by the suffering in the world? For example, let's imagine you pick up a magazine and learn that the waters of the world are increasingly polluted and scarce. One way to counteract the fear and helplessness that this news creates in you is to generate feelings of loving-kindness toward those who are suffering.

1   Sit in a comfortable position. Relax and quiet any mental chatter. Direct your breathing and attention toward your heart. Let a feeling of calm come over you.

2   When you're ready, bring to mind someone who is suffering. It could be the people in the world who live without access to food or clean water. Focus your loving attention on these people.

3   Now, breathe in and out from the region around your solar plexus, your chest area, your heart center. As you breathe from your heart center, generate a feeling of benevolence or kindness. Feel your heart soften. Now repeat these phrases in your mind:

May all beings in the world be safe, happy, and healthy.

May all beings be free from suffering.

Loving-kindness allows us to soften our hearts and have compassion for our shared humanity—we all suffer, we all long for happiness. When we water the seeds of good intentions rather than fear and hopelessness, we can actually imagine a safe, healthy world. If we don't water the seeds, they won't grow.

Three Paths to Letting Go

Forgiveness has great power. In this meditation you will ask for forgiveness from those you've harmed; you'll forgive those who've harmed you; and, last but not least, you'll learn to forgive yourself.

1   Begin this meditation by finding a comfortable position. Close your eyes and let your attention follow your breath. Let your breath be gentle and steady. Now think of someone you may have harmed; maybe you lashed out at a friend when you were in a bad mood. Say to yourself, either silently or aloud, "To those whom I've harmed, knowingly or not, I ask your forgiveness."

2   Next, bring to mind someone who has harmed you. Don't
    worry if you don't feel an immediate sense of love or even
    kindness for this person. You are setting your intention and
    having faith that you are capable of forgiving this person. Say
    to yourself, "For any harm that you have caused me, know-
    ingly or not, I forgive you."

3   Next, bring yourself to mind. Think of some small way
    you've been untrue to yourself or not lived up to your own
    expectations. Practice being kind and gentle with your fail-
    ings by saying to yourself, "For any ways that I have harmed
    myself, I offer forgiveness."

Over time you'll begin to notice that you hold less resentment
toward yourself and others.

Caught in the Web of Love

The idea that each individual is his own island—independent, in need of no one, solitary—is absurd. The reality is, we are all intricately connected by a web of relationships—to others, to the world that surrounds us, to the food that we eat. We wouldn't be alive if not for the kindness of others, and everything we do affects the world we live in.

We can begin to see that everyone deserves our affection. The next time you're out in the world, make it your practice to notice how you're connected to others. For example:

- If not for the bus driver, I wouldn't be able to get to work on time.

- Without my work, I wouldn't be able to feed my family.

- If not for the hard work of the farmers, I wouldn't have food on my table.

- If not for the trees in the forest, I wouldn't have a house.

- If not for the rain, there wouldn't be trees.

Our connection to the world around us is infinite. When you see a stranger, say to yourself, "May he be well." Repeat the phrase again and again until you feel genuine affection for this stranger. We can make caring for the welfare of others—strangers, loved ones, plants, animals, and ourselves—our main practice in life.

Be a Lover, Not a Fighter

You can make it your practice not to react defensively when provoked. Notice the times where you do feel like lashing out at someone or something: Your partner has left dirty dishes in the sink again. You hit every traffic light on the way to work when you're already late. Your mother tries to pick a fight at dinner.

Not fighting against everyone in sight doesn't mean that you're a passive doormat who lets the world wipe its shoes on you; it just means you notice your desire to fight the world, yet you lovingly choose not to do so. The next time something riles your emotions and you're tempted to lash out, send kindness toward the world instead. Say these phrases to yourself:

May we all be filled with loving-kindness.

May we be peaceful and at ease.

May we be happy.

If you can become aware of this desire to fight the world but not act on that desire, you may notice that these combative situations begin to disappear. With no one to fight, the battles end.

Soften Your Heart

The more you focus on loving-kindness within yourself, the more of this quality you'll have to offer others. The loving-kindness phrases can have a softening effect on your heart, bringing warmth, love, and tenderness for others. In addition, loving-kindness helps you form a more intimate relationship with yourself and lets you see that we're all connected in this world.

The next time you feel lonely and disconnected from the world around you, try this:

1　On the in-breath, say to yourself, "May I be safe, happy, and healthy, and live joyously."

2　On the out-breath, say to yourself, "May all beings be safe, happy, and healthy, and live joyously."

Repeat these sentences until you begin to feel kindness toward yourself and others. If you can't actually feel that, just practice saying the phrases. In many cases, the words are a gateway to the feeling of connection. You can also try this as a walking meditation, directing the phrases toward yourself for a few steps, and then directing them toward others.

Love Your Enemy

You don't have to like someone to love him. In order to truly experience compassion, you must learn how to direct goodwill not only toward those you like but also toward those you don't like.

Do you really want a person you don't like to experience infinite suffering? What good would that do? How can you wish suffering for one person while wishing that your own suffering be diminished? Isn't this a bit selfish?

If you can remember that we all experience pain, you can see that your enemy is no exception. Maybe if you wish him well, it will decrease the suffering he causes others. Maybe if he finds true happiness, he'll begin to treat others more kindly. In this way, you'd be contributing to the transformation of your enemy.

Think of someone who is causing harm in the world. It could be a political leader, a head of a major corporation, or simply someone with whom you work. Let's practice feeling love and compassion for this person by repeating the following phrases:

May you be free of pain and sorrow.

May you find peace.

May there be an end to your suffering.

Don't worry if a fountain of love doesn't spring up from within you. Just remember that kindness generates kindness, and that over time this practice will bring about change in how you relate to others, whether you like them or not.

Wrapped Up in Your Love

Let's dedicate this practice to those in the world who are struggling. It doesn't matter if you know them or not; it doesn't matter if you actually love them or not. The practice of offering love lets us become a force of compassion in a world filled with conflict and pain.

1   Find a comfortable position and begin to focus on your breath as it travels in and out through your nose. The point of following the breath is to enter the present moment and rest there.

2   Bring to mind someone who is suffering. It could be someone you know who is going through a medical crisis, or it could be a whole population of people, such as those who don't have enough to eat.

3   Visualize love traveling out of your own heart and encircling someone who is suffering. See this person wrapped up in your love like a baby in a blanket.

4   See this person smiling contentedly, secure in knowing that she is loved and cared for.

5   Make an offering to this person, such as "May you be free from harm and suffering. May you be well. May you feel safe and secure."

6   When you're ready, you can end this practice by gently moving your body.

You don't need to lock the doors to your heart when you end your formal practice. You can take this openhearted feeling of love for others with you throughout the day.

Conclusion

Going Forward

Loving-kindness doesn't end when you read the last line of this book; it can continue to be a part of your life for as long as you live. Why not make friends with yourself? Why not find a way to drop the negative self-talk and learn to trust the power of your own kindness? Why not let the wisdom that comes from this practice inform your life and free your mind?

We all have the gift of loving-kindness inside us. Loving-kindness meditation is a road map that shows us how to nurture and share this gift. Give yourself a chance to let this practice become a part of your inner life. As you let yourself feel your warmth and good-heartedness, your kindness will naturally spread out into the world.

We offer a deep bow to you for trying to bring loving-kindness meditation into your life. No matter what your effort has been, it's exactly what it needed to be. Once loving-kindness has touched your consciousness, it is hard to forget. Always know that in any situation, especially one of fear and worry, you now have a place you can rest your mind.

May you find peace.

May the wisdom of this practice penetrate your heart.

May all beings be well and happy.

May we each share our bright and wondrous nature for the benefit of all beings.

Resources

If you're interested in further exploring formal loving-kindness, also known as *metta* meditation, consider the following resources.

Meditation and Retreat Centers

Insight Meditation Society, Barre, MA, (978) 355-4378, www.dharma.org.

Spirit Rock Meditation Center, Woodacre, CA, (415) 488-0164, www.spiritrock.org.

Books on Loving-Kindness and Meditation

Brantley, Jeffrey. 2007. *Calming Your Anxious Mind*. Oakland, CA: New Harbinger Publications.

Boorstein, Sylvia. 2007. *Happiness Is an Inside Job*. New York: Ballantine Books.

Brach, Tara. 2004. *Radical Acceptance: Embracing Your Life with the Heart of a Buddha*. New York: Bantam Books.

Chodron, Pema. 2001. *The Places That Scare You*. Boston: Shambhala Publications.

Gunaratana, Henepola. 2001. *Eight Mindful Steps to Happiness*. Somerville, MA: Wisdom Publications.

His Holiness the Dalai Lama. 2003. *The Compassionate Life*. Somerville, MA: Wisdom Publications.

Kornfield, Jack. 1993. *A Path with Heart*. New York: Bantam Books.

————. 2003. *The Art of Forgiveness, Lovingkindness, and Peace*. New York: Bantam Books.

Nhat Hanh, Thich. 1997. *Teachings on Love*. Berkeley, CA: Parallax Press.

Salzberg, Sharon. 1995. *Lovingkindness: The Revolutionary Art of Happiness*. Boston: Shambhala Publications.

————. 1997. *A Heart as Wide as the World*. Boston: Shambhala Publications.

————. 2005. *The Force of Kindness: Change Your Life with Love and Compassion* (includes CD). Boulder, CO: Sounds True.

Prayer Beads

Loving-Kindness Prayer Beads; includes a CD teaching loving-kindness meditation. www.seedsofkindness.biz.

Research

Carson, James W. 2005. "Loving-kindness meditation for chronic low back pain." *Journal of Holistic Nursing* 23(3):287-305.

Fredrickson, B. L., Cohn, M. A., Coffey, K. A., Pek, J., and Finkel, S. M. 2007. "Open hearts build lives: Positive emotions, induced through meditation, build consequential personal resources." Manuscript under review.

Mary Brantley, MA, LMFT, teaches mindfulness-based stress reduction (MBSR) and loving-kindness meditation at Duke Integrative Medicine. She participated in a seven-day professional training in MBSR under the direction of Jon Kabat-Zinn, Ph.D., and Saki F. Santorelli, Ed.D. Brantley has practiced meditation for more than twenty-five years and attends yearly intensive retreats.

Brantley is a licensed marriage and family therapist who has maintained a private psychotherapy practice since 1983. She is co-owner of Seeds of Kindness, a business that makes loving-kindness prayer beads. You can learn more about Brantley's loving-kindness prayer beads at www.seedsofkindness.biz.

Tesilya Hanauer, CMT, is a freelance writer and certified massage therapist. She received her massage training at Heartwood Institute in northern California, where she also studied Iyengar yoga. She lives in the San Francisco Bay Area.